The Executive Secretary Guide to Taking Control of Your Inbox

Dr Monica E. Seeley

Marcham Publishing

Cover image by missimoinsane
http://missimoinsane.deviantart.com/

To my Goddaughters, Amy and Sula,
for keeping me young at heart.

Foreword by Sue France

In today's world of excessive emails, we need intelligent email handling rules, tips, techniques and advice to be in control of our time and sanity, and perform to the best of our ability.

Assistants have to be ultra-efficient in email management, especially if they look after more than one inbox. Their role is huge and email management is just one small part of it, albeit a very important part because you only need to miss or delete one email that you needed for mistakes to happen.

I enjoyed the way the book is written, which is like a story with 'Sophie' the executive assistant and 'Max' the email management genie. These characters make the book easy to read and you can identify yourself with Sophie and come to rely on 'Max's' intelligent expert answers. 'Max' makes suggestions in such a way you can choose which will work for you, your executive and your organisation.

There are many brain-friendly tips and advice within the book to help you with inbox management. If your executive looks after their own inbox, you can help them by setting up rules, folders and recommending best practice on how to deal with their emails and work out the best method for you to work with each other and manage each other's expectations.

You might even give your executive a copy of this book as the tips and advice are relevant to all email users, not just assistants.

I particularly like the advice on how to reduce the influx of often unnecessary emails, by re-educating your email senders to either stop sending, send to the correct person or speak to you direct! We are reminded that there are other methods of communication including a good old fashioned handwritten note that can really make an impression.

'Max's' law on sending emails and being able to stop email distraction is paramount to save time for you, as well as others, and will enable you to be able to focus your full attention where and when needed.

Through 'Max', Monica reminds us about proper email etiquette and that our emails are our 'digital dress code' – five key elements of which are all-important to gain the recipient's attention, make the right impression and show respect.

The summary of key points at the end of each chapter is helpful for recapping the salient advice and tools.

Sue France is a trainer, coach and author of The Definitive Personal Assistant & Secretarial Handbook and The Definitive Executive Assistant & Managerial Handbook.

www.suefrance.com

The role of paper in the digital age

Pukka - a slang-term used in British English to describe something as "first class" or "absolutely genuine".

The Urban Dictionary

It is not unusual for a child of five to have a digital device, so where does pen and paper fit in this digital age?

Did you know that we are 100 times more likely to remember information if we write it down with a pen on a traditional paper pad than on a digital device? Pen and paper in a meeting is less intrusive and distracting than a digital device. After all, it's harder to check your emails if you are making paper notes than it is on a digital tablet.

A paper notepad never runs out of juice, so there is never that embarrassing moment when you switch on your device only to find it dead. Talking of embarrassing situations, you can take you pen and pad anywhere including the bathroom, without it buzzing for your attention like a phone.

You can use many apps on a device but sometimes it is quicker and easier to doodle on a notepad, especially with lots of coloured pens.

These are some of the reasons why Pukka-Pads believe that pen and paper still have a very important role to play alongside technology and why we are delighted to sponsor this book.

When we started, my whole philosophy for the business (Pukka Pads) was to put some fun back into an industry which was male dominated and boring. We believe we have achieved that and nothing makes me happier than to see people using our product. Today we supply products for everyone from the very young to the very old. All our products are made from the highest quality paper from sustainable forests and are FSC certified.

Chris Stott, CEO, Pukka Pads

Jotta Polyprop
A4 / A5

Casebound Pad
A4 / A5

Wirebound Pad
A4 / A5

Flexi Pad
B5 / A5 / A6

Meeting Pad
A4+

Reporter's Pad

Box File
A4

Lever Arch File
A4

Ringbinder File
A4

Top Selling Products from Pukka Pads

Metallic Jotta A4/5

Stripes Project Book A4/5

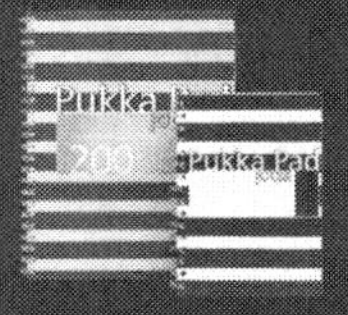

Navy Jotta Notepads

Contents

1

Introduction

The report of my death was an exaggeration.

Mark Twain

Taking Control of Your Inbox provides you with essential ways to manage your inbox and use email etiquette to save time to do the really important jobs, enjoy the things you love in life and impress those with whom you work. *Taking Control of Your Inbox* is based on a day in the life of an Assistant just like you and will help you handle the challenges you meet every time you look at your inbox.

This book is based on over 15 years' experience supporting business executives and their Assistants and office managers to reduce the volume of emails they need to deal with each day and communicate clearly through email to create good working relationships. It is packed with practical and pragmatic tips and advice.

Email was invented over 30 years ago, in 1971, by Ray Tomlinson, an American coder. It is one of the longest-surviving technologies and has become the staple diet of most business communications. Despite much talk of email being killed off by social-media-based technologies, it is here to stay in business, at least for the foreseeable future.

Email is a double-edged sword. It can save time and be a performance enhancer. Left untamed, though, it is one of the biggest drains on your performance and well-being. Indeed 'email addiction' is now recognised as a serious problem for businesses.

Receiving upwards of 50 emails a day is not unusual. That is about one new email every seven minutes during a normal working day. If you are managing not just your own inbox but also a second one too, you may need to handle 100-plus emails a day. Little wonder key emails can be overlooked. Replying in haste often initiates an email war. Worse still you often feel stressed and cannot conceive of switching off for fear of the tsunami of emails awaiting your return.

How you write email is your digital dress code (for example, how you greet the recipient, write the content and sign off). In less than three seconds, based on the look, tone and language in your email, the recipient has made up their mind how much value it will be for them to work with you.

By adopting a few basic principles of email best practice you can reclaim your life from the inbox, be confident that your emails convey a professional image of you and create good business networks.

You can read this book either from cover to cover or dip into the sections where you most need help. Either way I hope you enjoy this book and find it useful.

Dr Monica E. Seeley

2

Monday morning blues

The key is not to prioritize what's on your schedule, but to schedule your priorities.

Stephen Covey

Sophie works for an international engineering company and is executive assistant to the MD of the Sales Division Richard Hogan. She has a BSc in history and speaks fluent French. She is based in their London HQ although the company has three other offices in the UK and several around Europe, Australia, the Far East and America.

Sophie arrives at her desk just after 8.30 am on Monday morning to see over 25 new emails. Meeting madness on Friday means there are about 50 emails from last week too, which still need attention. Of these new and old emails she probably only really needs about 50 percent. The rest will be a mix of emails that either need to be read at some point or can be instantly deleted.

Sophie scanned the emails over the weekend and on the journey into her office. She decided they could probably all wait until arriving at the office, although leaving them did make her feel anxious. She has three meetings during the day and a long to-do list with several tasks that have now become urgent. Top priority is booking flights for Richard and a room with conference-call facilities for Friday. Add to that she is taking leave as of next week.

Sophie feels the stress mounting even though she spent the weekend trying to relax with a round of golf and time spent with friends and family.

Sounds familiar? Well Sophie (and you the reader) are in luck. Max the email management genie has just flown in from the 'Clean Inbox' kingdom. Max is visible only to Sophie, like those help bubbles which pop up when you are searching a website. Max used to be the CEO of a major international hi-tech organisation and is passionate about making effective use of email. Max is now a specialist in email best practice and ensuring that you control your working day rather than having email (and hence the inbox) controlling you.

Max will spend the day with Sophie coaching her how to save time and improve her well-being and performance. She is already a top EA although over the previous weeks, and unbeknown to her, Max has noticed scope for improvement.

The only thing Max asks in return is that Sophie provides food and especially chocolate, coffee and water at regular intervals.

Where do I begin?

Sophie opens her inbox and starts to deal with the sea of unopened emails. "Stop," shouts Max.

"Before you even open your inbox, create a to-do-list, prioritise the tasks and decide what must be done today."

Top of the list is booking flights and the conference call system. Max guides Sophie to quickly look at the inbox to make sure nothing has changed and then close it. "Now do those two tasks and then tick them off your list," he says.

Max comments that judging from other client's experiences, if anyone wants you that urgently they will find you. We can address the issues arising from anyone who does rely on email later in the day. By 9.15 am Sophie has completed the most urgent tasks for the day (thus far). It's time for a *pain au chocolat* and some coffee before they sort through the inbox.

Triage your inbox

With over 75 unread emails from Friday and today, Max tells Sophie that she must triage her inbox just as she would a hospital emergency ward. "Look for the 'must' emails," he says. "The objective is to **action the important emails before they become urgent and potential problems**." Here is Max's five point plan:

Monday morning clean up

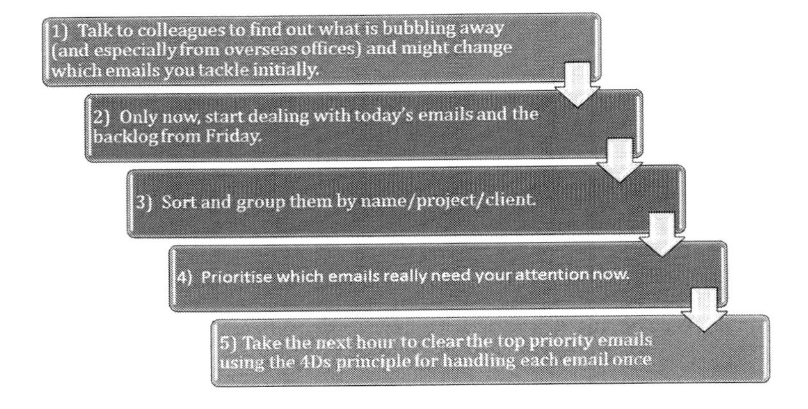

Prioritising

Priority management is the answer to
maximizing the time we have.

James C. Maxwell

There are all sorts of schemes to categorise emails, just as there are for the task list. Max says the key is to keep it as simple as 1-2-3 (or A/B/C). It must work for you. For email management, one method that many of Max's clients find most useful and easy to use is:

1. High – must respond now.
2. Medium – a response is required during the day.
3. Low – can wait until later in the week/not needed at all.

Alternatives are to sort by person/project/client, etc. Again, within these groups you need to prioritise from high to low.

"Now spend the next hour (meetings permitting) clearing the high and possibly the medium priority emails using the 4Ds principle for handling each email once (deal, defer, delegate or delete)," says Max. "This way your inbox becomes your work in hand rather than a dumping ground for every email you receive, and you find yourself trawling through it countless times to find what you need."

The 4D process for handling each email once

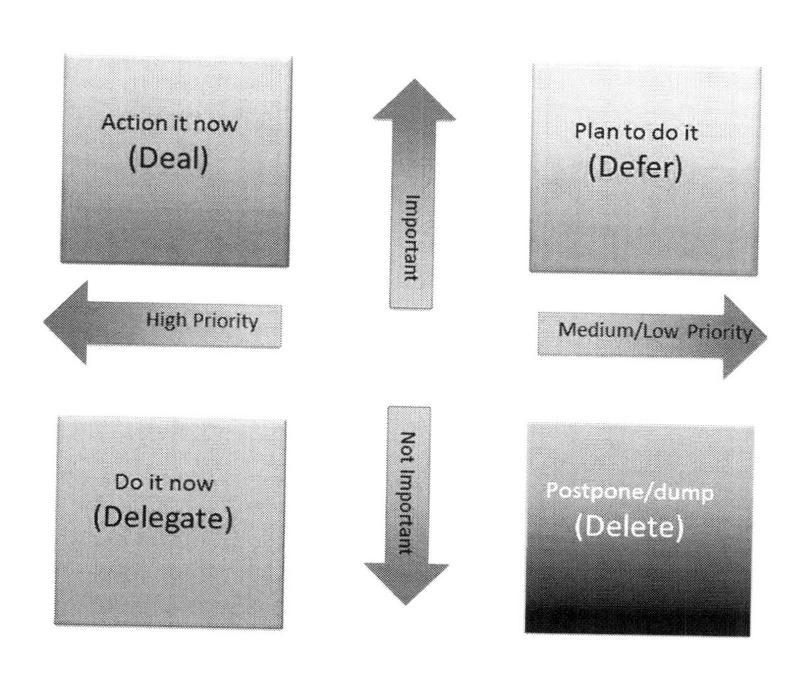

Whatever happens, Max stresses to Sophie, "Do not allow yourself to be distracted by incoming emails as this will mean that what is high priority and important becomes urgent and important and that is a recipe for more stress."

Handle each email once – 4Ds

Max recommends to Sophie a significant time saver: "**Don't just open an email thinking you will go back to it: do something with it**." Otherwise, he says, you will end up re-reading scores of emails as you forget what they were about and what you need to do. The principle of 4Ds is designed to enable you to handle each email once and once only. You must, Max advises, do one of the following:

- DEAL – high priority.
- DEFER – high/medium priority.
- DELEGATE – high/medium priority.
- DELETE – low priority.

Deal – do one of the following as appropriate: respond (and then either delete the original or file the response in the relevant folder); or read it and take no further action other than folder it.

Defer – the email needs a response but you cannot give one just yet. Put a reminder in it (see below for options) and if you are not going to respond within 24 hours let the sender know when to expect a response.

Delegate – a response is required soon but either you are not the right person to respond or someone needs to help you prepare the response. Forward it to them for help. You might want to keep tabs on the response using one of the options listed below.

Delete – everything which you really do not need.

Options for keeping tabs on emails which still need action include:

- Flags.
- Colour/Categories.
- Create a task/calendar entry.
- Mark as unread.

"Is any one of these better than the other?" asks Sophie.

"No, it's what works best for you," replies Max. "The only consideration is not to use too many reminders otherwise you become overwhelmed with red alerts, which again is stressful."

We will deal with ways to reduce the numbers of low priority (unimportant and not urgent) emails in Chapter 3 on reducing email traffic.

What if I don't have an hour to spare?

"Often it's a matter of checking my emails between meetings and other activities. Sometimes I only have 15 minutes. What do I do then?" asks Sophie.

"Ah," says Max. "It's still as simple as 1-2-3. You must apply the rules for prioritising and the 4Ds. But, in terms of the emails you deal with, pick those to which you can respond within a couple of minutes and leave those requiring a longer response until you have more time. Some call this the 'Swiss cheese' approach. You make inroads into all the high priority tasks in small bites (in this case emails). The list of Category 1, high priority emails does not look so daunting when you have proper quality time at your desk."

Working with multiple devices

After Sophie returns from a couple of meetings, Max notices that she is deleting and moving some emails that appear to be unread. "What's going on?" Max asks.

"Well," Sophie replies, "I have dealt with some of the more high priority ones during the meetings."

"Hmm, not a good idea," retorts Max almost in disgust."First, you should be staying focused on the meeting. Second, this is one of the biggest downsides of using mobile devices. Depending on how they are synchronised, it can mean you still need to folder the emails when you return to your main device (for example, your laptop)."

Indeed Max asserts that increasingly people are waiting until they return to their desk and main device rather than constantly checking emails on the go. It saves processing emails twice and having to clear up multiple mailboxes. Max suggests Sophie checks how her devices are synchronised and thinks about the most efficient one for handling her emails. For some it is a mobile device, for others the laptop/PC remains the best with a mobile device used judiciously.

More time – how does that happen?

Time is what we want most, but what we use worst.

William Penn

"Some days there is never a clear hour," complains Sophie.
Before responding Max looks carefully at Sophie's calendar. "Where is your 'me time'?" Max asks. Starting to feel a little annoyed, Sophie retorts by saying in a slightly cynical tone, "What do you mean 'me time'? Often even lunch is taken on the run between buildings and meetings."

"Well that's the point," says Max. "If you don't protect and manage your time everyone else will do it for you according to their needs rather than yours. Take a look at all the top executives' diaries. You will always find gaps dedicated to themselves to catch up. It might not overtly say 'me time' but you can be sure it will be there. It also means there is slack in the day if urgent matters crop up."

Max tells Sophie to start blocking out small chunks of time (30 to 60 minutes each day) when she is busy but busy doing her own things. She can call it what she likes – for example, admin, email management, thinking time, travel, maybe even 'meeting with myself'. These are some of the names Max has seen other people use. Max has seen those who block out such time at the start and end of the day. Sometimes it does get eaten up by other activities but at least it is there as a backstop.

Pomodoro technique for clearing a backlog of emails

Another technique people find very useful is the Pomodoro technique. You allocate a time, which you then break up into smaller chunks, traditionally of 25 minutes (smaller blocks also work). Take a five minute break between each chunk and mark up your progress (for example, ten emails actioned and foldered out of the 30 that need attention).

Invented by Francesco Cirillo (a German designer) he called it Pomodoro because he used a tomato shaped timer and Pomodoro is the Italian word for tomato.

It is based on the assumption that our productivity and concentration decreases after about 25 minutes. The break acts as a refresher and stimulus to re-boot our performance. It is a useful way to tackle a backlog of emails and especially those that have mounted up after time away from the office (for example, in meetings, training, on leave, etc).

Max feels this is also a very sound way of limiting the risk of making a mistake because you are getting tired, rushing, losing concentration etc.

Resetting the priorities

Clearly as the day progresses priorities may change and you need to reflect on this when you do spend quality time working through your emails. "So do I have to triage my inbox again during the day?" asks Sophie.

"Yes," Max replies. "And **review the priorities for the emails left from the last session and keep applying the 4Ds principle for handling each email once and only once**. This way you should have a relatively clean inbox with maybe no more than 20 on-going emails in it. If you can reach an empty inbox even better, but that can be hard in the 24x7x365 world of global business. The main point is not to let the emails mount up in a random state of read and unread."

Sophie has written extensive notes in her Pukka Pad Project Book because she fears she may not remember all

Max's words of wisdom. Also she is sure she will want to share some of Max's advice with her colleagues and Richard the MD.

Summary – key points

- Do the important stuff before you even open your inbox. Check if necessary that nothing has changed but never let new emails throw you off course.
- Triage your emails (inbox) before you start to tackle them. Prioritise what needs your attention here and now, taking note of what else is going on in the office, which might change where you need to focus your attention.
- Don't allow important emails to build up to the point that they become important + urgent = stress.
- Use the 4Ds and always do something with each email as you read it, even if you only move it out to a folder for reference.
- Adopt a fool-proof way for keeping tabs on emails that still need attention.
- Assign quality (me) time in your calendar to deal with your email and at least at the start and end of the day. This is protected time when you do not go to meetings.
- When time is short, deal with the top priority emails in between other activities.

3

Reduce the unnecessary email traffic

I have a theory about the human mind.
A brain is a lot like a computer. It will only take so many facts,
and then it will go on overload and blow up.

Erma Bombeck

As the morning progresses Max notices how much email Sophie is deleting. "Why are you deleting so many of the emails you receive? Do you not need them? Do you trust your memory such that once read you will remember them?"

"They are all unnecessary. They are either of no interest to me or I have already seen them in my manager's inbox, which I keep an eye on," responded Sophie. "Worse still, some are from colleagues sitting just behind me and are about trivia.

"The problem is I don't really know how to stop these unnecessary emails entering my inbox in the first instance. Also it can mean I delete an important email in the process of deleting all the rubbish," sighs Sophie.

Max smiles wryly. "Email overload is the disease of 21st century office life. There is an endemic 'cover my backside' culture in most offices. Everyone copies everyone in on every email. Deleting is just not a solution; it wastes even more of your valuable time."

Also, unlike popular free online email providers like Google and Microsoft, most businesses limit the size of people's inboxes in order to maintain speed of service and contain the cost of running the email service. Therefore it is important that you manage and maintain a slim inbox.

"Let's start by looking at some numbers and the cost to you (and your MD). Then we will find ways to reduce the number of unwanted emails (internal spam, noise, junk... Call them what you will) and changing your colleagues' email behaviour and especially those who sit near you" says Max

Time wasted on unwanted emails

Most people only need between 40 and 60 percent of the emails they receive. Dealing with unwanted emails is one of the major time thieves because often you need to scan them to realise they are not relevant.

Here is the template Max suggests Sophie uses to estimate the cost of the unnecessary emails.

	Your inbox	Your manager
Total number of emails received per day		
Number which are unnecessary each day		
Time wasted per day = number of unwanted x 1.5 minutes		

To cost the total days and money per year use the Mesmo Consultancy Online Cost of Email Misuse Calculator at

http://www.mesmo.co.uk/assess-yourself/calculator/

Sophie estimates that on a typical day she receives 60 emails of which 30 are useless. These cost her 45 minutes to clear. This is half a day a week (21 days a year) just spent dealing with stuff she didn't request and does not need. It is similar for her manager, whose inbox she sometimes manages when he is away. This level of unnecessary email is not unusual in business today.

Over the year, therefore, Sophie herself receives about 6,300 unnecessary emails. As she manages her MD's box that figure might rise to 13,000 unwanted emails. Imagine if that were unsolicited paper junk mail? That would be between 6,300 and 13,000 envelopes to be opened, scanned and thrown in the rubbish bin. "You would soon start to take action to reduce the waste," Max says sympathetically.

"What would you do with the time you might save?" Max asks Sophie.

"Go home on time and disconnect," she replies instantly. So let's make it happen by preventing all those useless emails ever reaching your inbox. It might not happen overnight but over a few weeks we can certainly reduce the email traffic significantly.

Be ruthless: prioritise to reduce the waste

"Long live the Pareto Principle," says Max.

"What on earth is that?" says Sophie feeling a little threatened. "Does it come in different flavours? Is it a new diet?"

The Pareto Principle means that 80 percent of the information you need to perform your job comes from 20 percent of the emails you receive. We need to identify that 20 percent and eliminate the other 80 percent, which are wasting your time. Audit your inbox and decide what emails you need and where they need to arrive – in your inbox or directly in a folder. It's a five-step process.

The inbox audit process

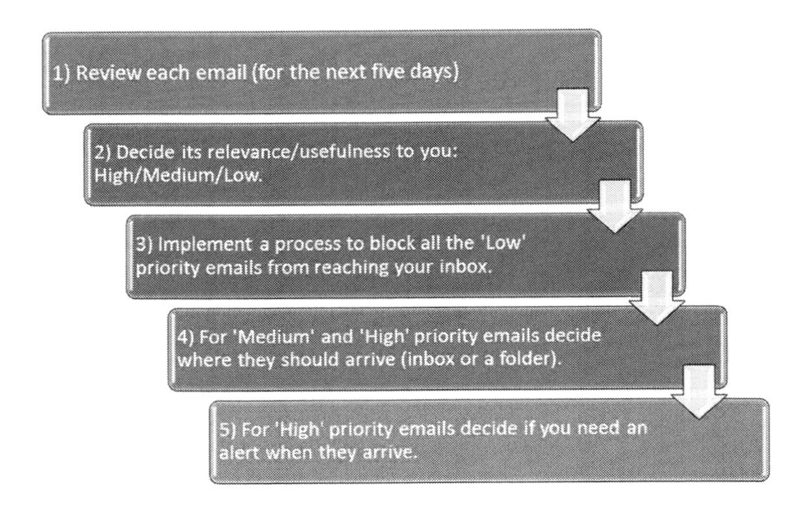

Here are some ways to remove the unnecessary low priority emails and manage the medium to high priority emails.

Low priority emails

These are those that you generally delete. Here are some ways to either stop them coming into your inbox or at least reduce the way they distract your attention from the important emails.

Assassinating low priority emails from your inbox

Sources	Possible actions
Cc'd emails	Ask to be removed from the mailing list. Write a rule to send them directly to another folder (in which you store Cc'd emails).
Duplicates of those you see in your manager's inbox but don't need yourself	Discuss with your manager who needs what and then tell the senders what needs to be sent to whom.
Newsletters	Ask to be removed from the mailing list (unsubscribe). Write a rule to send them directly to the deleted folder.
Social round robins e.g. celebration cakes, testing the fire alarm, sandwich lady is here etc.	Suggest the sender uses an alternative media – see Chapter 7 for more ideas. Write a rule to send them directly to the deleted folder.

Max tells Sophie that many expert users filter out the Cc'd emails so that they only see emails sent directly to them. They then check the Cc'd email folder once a day just to be quite sure there was nothing important.

Medium and High Priority emails

"Now it's very important to decide whether or not you need to see all these in your inbox. Alternatively, automatically have them sent to a folder which you can scan as and when you have time, for example newsletters, meeting invite responses, out of office messages etc." says Max.

Where should your emails arrive?

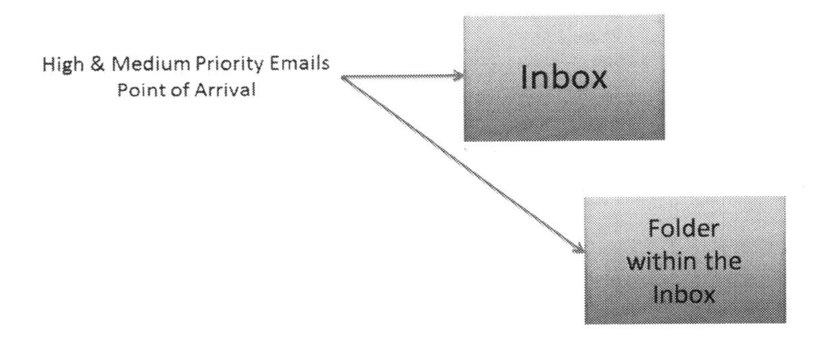

Alerts for high priority emails

For high priority emails, you might want to consider having an alert. Despite saying you should not be distracted by new emails, sometimes it is useful (maybe important) to know when your manager/key client has sent you an email. The form of the alert will depend on your email software. For instance with Outlook you can write a rule with a sound as the alert.

Typical examples of high priority emails, which you might send directly to a folder, are project related. For example, you may be focused on a specific project (A) but have emails coming in related to another highly visible project (B). However you will not be dealing with those from project B until later in the week. Max says clients often use a rule to divert emails automatically – in this case to a folder relating to project B. This again reduces distractions and helps maintain focus. The folder for project B can be reviewed at a specific time during the day to ensure there is nothing vital that cannot wait until the next day.

Max suggests that, after a week or so, Sophie should take another look at the medium priority emails, and re-audit them to see if there is further scope to reduce them.

Max adds, "Now you have at least one way by which you can reduce the volume of email traffic flowing through your inbox. It's a little like introducing a toll road for emails. We only allow the medium to high priority emails through the main inbox highway. The rest are automatically consigned to the B roads – that is, the deleted folder."

Reduce the emails you send

Max notices that Sophie often sends short emails just saying "thanks". In return she then receives one saying something along the lines of "my pleasure". She often also suddenly fires off several emails to the same person in quick succession.

"Do you realise that the more emails you send the more you receive?" says Max, shocked at Sophie's reckless use of email and her time. Although sending an email costs you no money it does cost you time – time to compose and time to reply. ***Think before hitting send*** is one of Max's laws of email best practice.

Here are some of the ways that Max has observed others apply this law and that he suggests Sophie can adopt in order to reduce the number of emails she sends:

- Question what value your email is adding for the recipient and you.
- Include a 'thank you' line in the original email and only send a follow-up gratitude email if really necessary. More in Chapter 11.
- Pause before hitting send to check that you have asked all the right questions/given the recipient sufficient information. If you are unsure, hold off for a while.
- Reduce the number of people to whom you send the email (in both the 'To' and 'Cc' address line).
- Accept that not every email either warrants or needs a reply. For example, when someone sends you some information, you do not have to send a thank-you email. When asked to do something, don't waste time and energy sending an email saying "OK". Wait until you have done what was asked and then reply (if necessary) – for example, book a room, compile some data.
- Challenge yourself as to whether or not email is the best way to convey this information. More in Chapter 7.

As the hours pass, Sophie becomes much more judicious with the 'Send' button. There is a marked reduction in the number of emails Sophie sends and hence receives.

Summary

- Calculate how much time you waste dealing with unnecessary emails (for you and your manager). Simply deleting unwanted emails is not the solution as this can cost and eat up to 45 minutes a day of your time, which could be better used.
- Apply the Pareto Principle to identify the 20% of the emails you receive which contribute 80% of what you need (to know/action). Audit your incoming emails (and your manager's) over a week and prioritise all incoming emails into one of three categories:
  - High (important must have)
  - Medium (useful but do not necessarily need to see immediately) and
  - Low (unnecessary do not need, will be deleted).
- Take action to prevent all low priority (unnecessary emails) from reaching your inbox. This can include using a rule to send them directly to the deleted folder).
- Control where the high and medium emails arrive (directly either in the inbox or a folder).
- Consider whether or not you need an alert when certain high priority emails arrive.
- Always think before hitting send and consider:
  - What value your email adds for you and the recipient. If there is none, then don't bother; and

- Is there a more effective way to interact with the other person? Yes? Then use it.

- Be judicious about how many emails you send. Reduce the number of names in both the 'To' and 'Cc' line. Sending fewer emails to fewer people means you receive fewer emails.

4

Don't get distracted by new emails

One way to boost our willpower and focus is to manage our distractions instead of letting them manage us.

Daniel Goleman

While Sophie is preparing for her 11.30 meeting Max notices something very strange. Her laptop keeps going ping and a small box floats across her screen. She immediately stops her preparation and opens her inbox. The new arrival seems either to delight or cause some angst. Either way she stops what she's doing immediately and deals with it, just like she would for a real emergency such as a fire.

The result is that Sophie short-changes herself on the time she has for reading the notes and rehearsing her presentation. This is an important meeting for Sophie in her role as a Well-being Champion for her division. So she ends up arriving a few minutes late and not quite as well prepared as she wanted. Nonetheless Sophie scrapes by, but wishes she had remembered to bring the absentee figures from the past quarter.

"'What happened?" Max asks. "You allocated one hour for preparation but in the end had just about fifteen minutes of quality time."

"People just expect me to be sitting watching my inbox for new emails (even in meetings). They expect an instant response," Sophie replies.

"Do they really expect an instant reply or is this your perception?" asks Max. "Furthermore, what is the cost of all these distractions to you?"

"You know Max, most days I feel like the inbox runs my day, but I am not sure how to change things," says Sophie.

Max takes a large bite of chocolate as he prepares to help Sophie become more productive and change the habit of a lifetime.

Distractions are expensive

Max explains that, over the past decade, countless studies have shown that you pay a high price for being distracted by new emails, even if you only glance at them:

- ***Fifteen minutes is what each email distraction adds to the time needed to complete the original task in hand because it interrupts your train of thought, even if only momentarily.***
- Hewlett Packard's 2005 study found email distraction can cause a ten point reduction in IQ.
- Creativity drops as you become immersed in the small things and fail to see the big picture.

- Concentration flies out the window and you lose focus on what you were doing.
- Mental energy drops.
- Stress levels rise up as you try to keep up with the day's task list.

"We are hopeless at multitasking, which is exactly what we are doing when we continuously deal with our email whilst doing other things," says Max. This is despite the fact that many people, especially among the younger generation, will peer at the screen while undertaking any number of other activities.

The most productive, creative and often healthiest people are those who can maintain focus, even if it's only for a short period. They disconnect from their inbox while they attend to the task in hand whether that be for five or 55 minutes.

Focus and stop all those new email distractions

Here are Max's top five tips to help Sophie stop being distracted by email. Following these will give her a chance to finish tasks on time and more time to think and do the things that really matter.

Stop the email interruptions

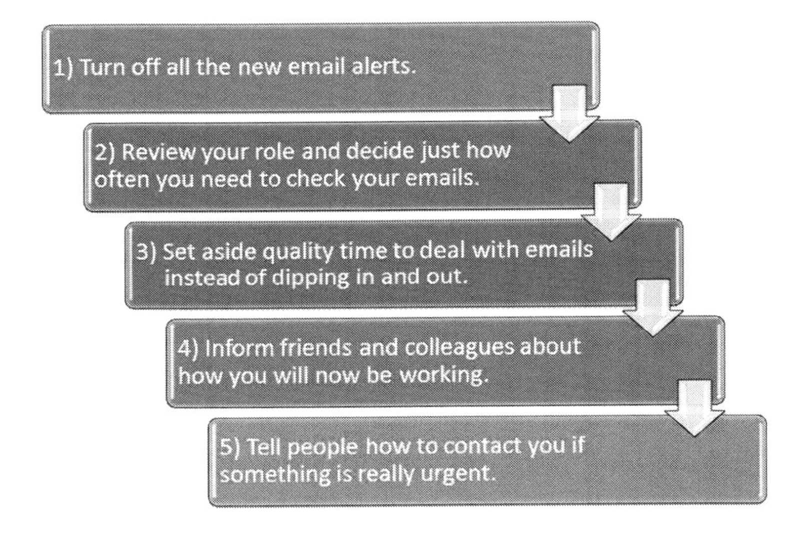

Max is adamant that Sophie turns off all the new email alerts, from the dreaded ping to the floating pop-up box, except for the high priority ones. Some people even disconnect and close their inbox completely when working on a task which needs a high level of concentration, creativity, etc., adds Max.

What is a reasonable time to step away from the inbox?

"That is fine," says Sophie. "But in reality what is a reasonable time to expect people, especially senior executives, to wait for a reply?" Max explains that it all depends on your role and relationship with the sender. If you are a front line worker, for example, in sales, it might be 30 minutes. If you are more of a back-office support person it could be up to half a day.

A working day is a rule of thumb during which all emails that need a response should receive one. Clearly this is something you need to discuss and agree with your manager and those with whom you work most closely to agree what is best for your role and business. The key is to move away from feeling you must reply instantly to each email and that each email even warrants a reply.

There will always be unusual situations where instant responses are needed, typical examples being lawyers during a takeover bid, and preparing a presentation to meet a deadline. However even in these situations you should ask yourself if an instant response is a reasonable expectation. After all, in the first example, the response may need to be considered and substantive, and hence take time to compile. In the second instance, better planning might have avoided working to a tight deadline.

Managing expectations

The goal is to work toward a world where expectations
are not set by the stereotypes that hold us back,
but by our personal passion, talents and interests.

Sheryl Sandberg

It is vital to manage the sender's expectation of when you will reply. Bear in mind too that your email behaviour will influence the other person's email behaviour.

The quicker you reply to an email, the quicker the other person will always expect a reply. It is interesting that our perception of what is expected is often different from the sender's. Max has observed that:

- Senior people often expect to wait a few hours and are surprised when they do receive a quick reply. Indeed it makes them wonder what other work the responder has to do!
- External senders are often prepared to wait longer than internals.
- Mobile device users often have unrealistic expectations.

At the end of the day, few emails are so urgent that waiting a few hours for a reply becomes a matter of life or death. If something was that urgent, you can be sure someone would contact you by another means. Max suggests there are several well-tried and trusted ways Sophie can start to manage her colleagues' expectations of when to receive a reply (internal and external).

- Do nothing and wait and see who chases. Then tell them about her new email regime.
- Add a line in your signature.
- Talk it through at team meetings, etc.
- Make it clear how to contact you if it is urgent (for example, text, phone, instant messenger if used).
- Use an auto response (or out-of-office message), which acknowledges the email and tell the sender you will deal with it and who to contact if it is really urgent.

The latter is an extreme measure but useful if you are either under pressure or in meetings all day.

Max says many of his clients are amazed at how much more work they complete after turning off all the new email alerts. They feel less stressed, and more in control of their lives, not to mention the inbox. Have they lost any business? No. If anything they gain as the sender sees a well organised business.

What if the email requires a substantial response?

Not all emails are equal. Some are easy to answer within your designated time frame. Others need you to collect data, think through what to say, be checked by colleagues, etc. For these more difficult ones, Max says, "Send a holding response, acknowledging receipt of the email and saying when you will respond in full." That way you have managed the sender's expectation, while giving them confidence that they will receive a professional robust response in due course.

Summary – key points

- Take control of your time, energy and day. Don't let email sap your energy.
- Switch off all those new email alerts (from the ping to the floating box).
- Establish a time period during which you will respond (from 24 minutes to 24 hours).
- Not all emails are equal. For difficult ones that will take longer to answer manage the sender's expectation by

acknowledging them and saying when they can expect a full response.

- Make people aware of how to contact you if the matter is urgent.

5

To folder or not to folder

I'm quite an untidy person in a lot of ways. But order makes me happy. I have to have a clear desk and a tidy desktop, with as few visual distractions as possible. I don't mind sound distractions, but visual ones freak me out.

Joanne Harris

Sophie has just dealt with a stack of emails and now the dilemma is what to do with them. Moving emails to a folder or just leaving them in the inbox is one of the most contentious elements of good email management. Sophie's inbox should be her work in hand. Sophie's goal is to see what still needs attention and what is new.

Max's advice is simple, ***put all emails which are complete in a relevant folder***. Why, you might ask, when most email software (Gmail and Outlook, for instance) provides you with massive storage space and fast search engines? How you manage your personal social email account is one thing. If you don't mind wasting precious social time scrolling through your bulging personal inbox and getting distracted as you spot other emails that is up to you. In the office, though, it is all about efficiency and compliance. This is where a good folder structure wins hands down.

Why bother?

"I'm already time poor," says Sophie. "Isn't this a chore, which adds no value to my overall performance?"

"Wrong," pipes up Max. A good inbox folder structure means:

- Emails are easier to find because a well-organised inbox is easier to search than a random one.
- It provides a space to park emails which do not require your immediate attention.
- You can brief yourself for a meeting more efficiently by going to one folder and checking all the related emails rather than scanning many thousands.
- You can manage the risk of a breach of compliance. When you add an email to a folder you can spot emails which should be deleted – more in Chapter 14.
- A good folder structure and process reduces the risk of missing an important email. It will help you keep your inbox small and hence you can see the trees from the woods, unlike keeping all your email in the main inbox.

"OK, I am slowly becoming a convert but I am still not quite sure as it can be fiddly. Sometimes emails fall into the wrong folder," says Sophie.

What is a good folder structure?

Max says, "Imagine it's an old fashioned filing cabinet, where you might file your music, store good wine, or sort your clothes, and so on. Would you randomly pile your socks on top of your dress and jeans? You would probably at the very least group items according to type. So too with emails in folders."

Max shows Sophie what his looks like. Under each main folder are some sub-folders. For example 'Clients' has a folder for each client, 'Travel' has one for each major trip, etc.

Folder structure

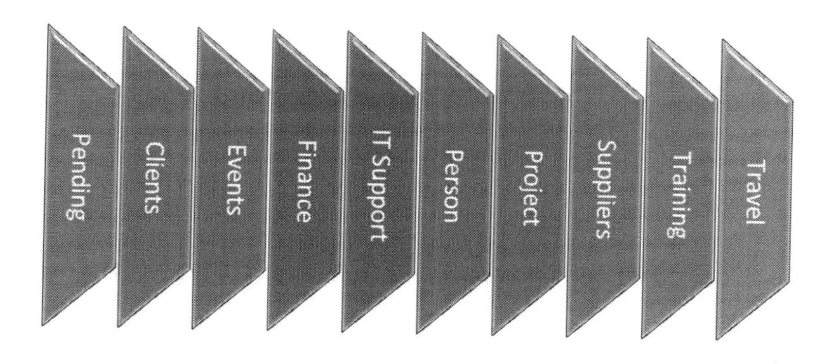

What's the 'pending' folder?

"Ah," replies Max smiling. "That's for all emails which either don't have a permanent place or are about matters to which I may or may not want to respond, events which might be interesting, etc." Indeed Max has several folders under pending:

- Meetings
- Leads/people to chase
- Old emails – left over from periods of leave, which might need attention.

Max has observed that really good Assistants often use their pending folder like a brought forward file. They have a sub-folder for each week/month, which they check at the start of that period – for example, a week.

Simpler folder structures

My filing system is messy but orderly.

Tony Benn

Max admits that some people have less detailed folder structures with just two or three subfolders – for example:

- Year – one for each year.
- Completed – for all emails which are fully actioned (even just read and the content digested).

Anything in the inbox by default is on-going and still needing attention. Observations indicate that such simple structures do appear to work for their owners although Max says “it can still be like looking for a needle in a haystack”.

When is the best time to do my filing?

There are two choices:

1. Once you have DEALT with the email. File the last email in the chain, which closes off the conversation: either the one you sent or the one you received. If the conversation goes on for some time, file after four/five iterations, remembering to delete the previous ones as you do so.
2. In batches. At either the end of the day or every three/four days.

In a busy week it is often a mix and match process. Max has seen some inboxes with 3,000+ emails. The important thing is to keep on top of it and not end up with an inbox with weeks if not months of unfiled emails. Then inbox maintenance becomes a chore and you quickly spiral in to taking no action and having thousands of unsorted emails in your top inbox folder.

What about days when a deluge of emails comes in relating to one specific topic?

"You mean like just now, when ten emails arrived relating to next month's away day?" asks Max.

"Yes," responds Sophie.

"Easy," continues Max. "Move them, and any others that come in during the day, out to the relevant folder immediately. Later in the day take a quick look at them to make sure none need an urgent response. When you are ready to deal with the task (the away day), open that folder just as you would a traditional one. Read them, see the whole picture and deal with them all accordingly."

Archiving files and all that jazz

"Hmm," sighs Max. "Overweight mailboxes can be a minefield awaiting an explosion." There are basically two types of 'archive' procedures, he explains:

1. Archiving software such as Enterprise Vault by Symantec and Mimecast from Mimecast. Emails are archived at regular intervals and saved in a place separate to your email whilst being accessible through your normal email software. Many organisations deploy such systems to enable them to locate old emails even after a person has left and for compliance purposes – for example, to answer Freedom of Information Act enquiries.

2. PST files. These are specific to Microsoft Outlook and are stored on your PC/laptop's hard drive. Again they can be accessed from your regular Outlook email. Some use them to reduce mailbox sizes. However PST files carry a major health warning. They are not stable over a certain size and if your PC crashes they may be lost forever. Far better is to reduce the volume and size of emails.

Sophie has been with her organisation for just over six months, but during that time she has never needed to find any really old emails. She believes they have a dedicated archiving system like her previous company. She thinks Richard her executive (the MD) is *au fait* with whatever they use. She knows she really ought to check exactly what process they have and how to use it and what is their retention policy. It's one more thing for her action list.

Using a mobile device: What happens to your folders?

This can be a downside as you may not be able to see all your folders. Today, however, most devices synchronise your main PC with your mobile device (including the folder structure), says Max. There is also software (called Good), which enables you to not only synchronise the folders but also select which ones you see on your mobile device. For example, you may choose not to see those folders with circulars and newsletters. However, depending on the device and software you cannot always move emails to folders from a mobile device. To her to-do list Sophie adds going to talk to the IT department about what they recommend as best practice from a process perspective for folders and synchronisation.

Max says, "You want to **avoid dealing with the same email on different devices, reading it on your mobile device then foldering it on your laptop.** For many this acts as an incentive to deal with their emails only when they are sitting at their laptop rather than on the move when accidents happen – like sending emails in haste or, at worst, walking into a passing car whilst emailing. Yes that has happened."

Summary

- A good folder structure is a balancing act.
- Keep the folder structure simple and meaningful to you. Too complicated and you will start to lose items. Indeed if you only have a couple of emails in a folder it suggests you need fewer folders for that topic/project.

- If it is too basic it may still leave you searching for a needle in a haystack.
- Folder your emails little and often. Keep your main inbox down to no more than two screens of live emails.

6

Handling the manager's inbox

Women have always ruled my life, be it my mother, my wife, my assistant, or my daughter, so I don't really fight with them. I relinquished control years ago.

Jon Bon Jovi

Sophie also oversees her manager Richard's inbox, especially when he is away from his desk/the office in meetings and on leave. She checks it every hour or so even though Richard has a mobile device (iPhone) on which he too checks his email.

Before lunch, Sophie says to Max that it is not the easiest of tasks. There are no clear guidelines as to what she should action, what Richard really wants to see and, indeed, what she should delete and file. Meeting invites and responses too can sometimes pose problems. The result is often duplication of effort as they both read the same emails. Worse still, some emails are answered twice and some fall between the two of them and are overlooked completely. Once this caused quite a commotion as the sender was an important client.

Max asks Sophie very pointedly, "Have you ever discussed how Richard expects you to manage his inbox? And, conversely, have you suggested how you can help him?" Max suggests the following general aspects to discuss with Richard:

- What are his priorities for the week (even day)?
- What is the best way for you draw important emails to Richard's attention?
- Do you know whether or not he likes you to delete and file his emails?
- What protocols are in place when Richard is on leave?

"I've never discussed this with Richard," admits Sophie. "I thought it would be intuitive and suspect he thought the same. After all, using email is meant to be second nature in business."

Max throws his hands in the air and takes a long drink of water before commenting. "But how can it be intuitive? It is like trying to read the other person's mind and second guess what they want to eat when you do not even know if they are vegan, or like red or white wine, and so on," says Max.

Max smiles and says that handling your manager's email is just another aspect of the working relationship that needs care and attention for it to be successful. "And there are plenty of ways we can throw light on the dark matter in your manager's inbox to make life much more effective for you both," he adds.

Talk, talk and talk again about what your manager needs

The foundation for handling another person's inbox is to discuss and review expectations as priorities and the nature of the business change. The practice and protocols are really identical to those already discussed for managing your own inbox, says Max, but in this case, the focus of attention is the manager and their preferred way of working.

Max offers Sophie a template of questions and topics to discuss with Richard at their next catch-up meeting later in the day. Normally this happens at the start of the week but was postponed as Richard had an important client to meet.

Aspect	Who is responsible/ process
Prioritising incoming emails – what is important to the manager and how do they like to be notified?	
Urgent/important emails – should the Assistant send a holding response?	
Low priority emails (those normally deleted). Who takes responsibility for taking the manager off the distribution list?	
Meeting invites – does the manager need to see these?	
Duplicate email, both sent the same email (one in the To and one in the Cc line) - is this necessary or can one of them be taken off the distribution list?	
Confidential emails.	
Foldering/filing – who makes sure it happens?	
Keeping the overall inbox within limits (where applicable)?	
Archiving old emails (again where applicable)?	

Clearly the protocols and processes will depend on a number of factors and not least the manager's personal level of email IT fitness (email software skills); seniority; and how often they travel and are unable to access their emails. Yes, some managers are far less skilled than their Assistants, perhaps as a result of their age and maybe because it just does not interest them. Some senior executives just expect their Assistants to manage their inbox while others are happy to deal with it entirely themselves. The spectrum is wide and Max has seen a multitude of variations on a theme. Here are some processes that have proved useful for the Assistants with whom Max has worked.

Prioritising

This is best done by reviewing what is important for the manager each week/month. If as Assistant you are in charge of the inbox it can be very valuable to do an inbox audit (as we did in Chapter 3 to reduce the email traffic in your own inbox). This will **make it very clear how much time you are wasting dealing with your manager's inbox and how much time others are wasting sending the manager emails he may never read.**

In one case, a manager with whom Max worked was regularly copied in on emails by his team but actually saw less than 50 percent of them.

Typical executive's inbox and percentage of emails they deal with themselves

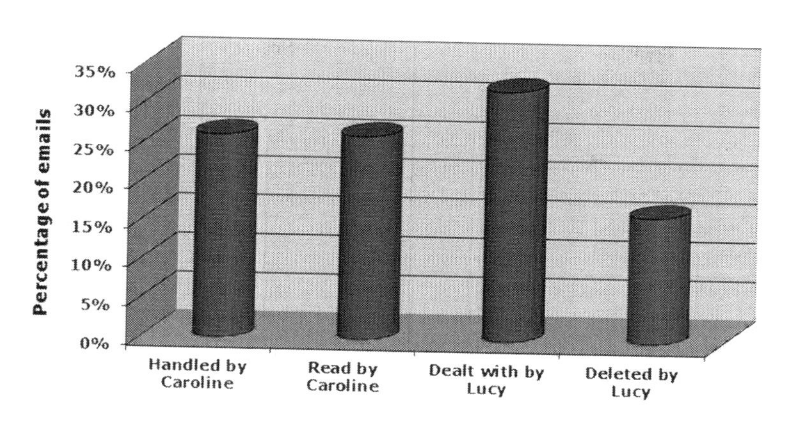

In a typical executive's inbox (as shown in the figure above), the Assistant (Lucy) either deals with the emails or deletes them because she knows her director (Caroline) would not want to see them. Caroline showed her team just how many of the emails they sent her which she never saw (just over half). She then explained what she really wanted to see. This rapidly reduced the email traffic through her inbox and hence the demand on Lucy's time dealing with email.

Important/urgent emails – how to draw attention to them

Options include:

- Flag them in the inbox on their PC (if that is where the manager usually deals with their emails).
- Put in a separate folder – for example, called 'Urgent'. This option assumes the manager sees his folders either via his PC or mobile device.

- Respond and forward the response to the manager with something in the subject line to attract their attention – for example, 'Urgent'. This is good for managers who deal with their email primarily from their mobile device.
- Text the manager with details of which emails need their immediate attention. This is really useful because interestingly we often see our texts and phone messages before our email.

Much clearly depends on whether or not the manager checks their emails on a mobile device whilst on the go and their personal preference.

Low priority emails

This is perhaps the trickiest one. **Some managers hate to delete anything, even the most trivial emails** – for example, the fire alarm is being tested. Others are happy to have all the useless emails deleted by their Assistant.

The key is to understand your manager's neurosis and make suggestions accordingly. One way is to move all the emails that are potential candidates for deletion to a holding folder. This is good for those who like to keep every email.

Meeting invites

Again Max has seen a variety of techniques for moving these out of the manager's inbox so that they do not obscure the important emails. These often depend on the software being used.

- Send the invite from your mailbox and hence have the replies come directly to you.

- Send the invite from the manager's inbox but have replies directed to you.
- Filter out all meeting-related responses using rules.

Which works best will also depend on how much control you have over the manager's calendar and access levels to their inbox. For security reasons, some organisations place restrictions on the level of delegation.

Confidential emails

Historically, privacy was almost implicit,
because it was hard to find and gather information.
But in the digital world ... we need to have more explicit rules –
not just for governments but for private companies.

Bill Gates

Although Assistants are usually the manager's most trusted confidant, **there are times when you may not wish to see certain (confidential) emails** sent to your manager – for example, a colleague being made redundant, a takeover bid, etc. **These need to be filtered out.**

Options here, which Max has seen implemented and that protect Assistants from being party to emails they are not comfortable seeing are:

- Filter out to a folder. This relies on the emails having the words 'Confidential' in the subject-line. Senders must be aware of this process and adopt the protocols.
- Have a separate email account to which only the manager has access.

Again the choice will depend on the organisation and email systems in use.

Foldering/Archiving/Keeping within mailbox limits

Max says this is very much a personal choice, which Sophie and her manager must make. The only criteria are to stick to what has been agreed, otherwise it's a recipe for disaster. There are three basic models for managing the inbox in terms of who is in control:

1. *Chauffeured* – you manage the inbox and just draw to their attention what they must personally handle. You do all the filing (foldering), deleting, and responding to, run of the mill emails and handle all meeting invites.

2. *Named driver* – it's a joint approach and together you work the inbox. This means having a clear agreement on what and when you deal with their emails.

3. *Owner driver* – the manager deals almost exclusively with their emails and inbox, and only asks you to take charge when they are on leave.

Given that most managers have mobile devices, the named driver approach seems most common whereby you both do some of the inbox housekeeping. Implicit in that approach is that you must both agree on a folder structure that works for the manager. You can advise about sound folder structures but Max adds that some Assistants meet resistance from managers who either just don't believe in using folders or feel they are above having a mailbox limit: "In such cases all you can do is chip away slowly to change bad behaviour!"

"Clearly," Max continues, "The way the inbox is managed, like all other aspects of the Assistant-manager relationship, needs to be reviewed periodically and changed as required to maintain performance."

"Good point," says Sophie. "I will add a reminder to my next one-to-one meeting with Richard to review how I manage his inbox. The timing is excellent as he is due to go travelling for two weeks."

"Time for lunch," exclaims Max.

Summary

- The primary goal is to ensure that all emails are handled once and once only.
- Agree how and who reduces unnecessary email traffic.
- Reduce duplication wherever possible – that is, if you both receive the same emails and emails are reviewed and handled by you both, such as meeting invites and discussions in which you are copied in.
- Manage the risk of emails being overlooked by both of you.
- Agree a process for highlighting important emails that need the manager's attention.
- Have a protocol in place for handling sensitive and confidential emails.
- Establish who is primarily responsible for doing any necessary email housekeeping – for example, foldering, deleting and archiving old emails.

7

Think outside the inbox

Listening is a positive act: you have to put yourself out to do it.

David Hockney

Returning from lunch, Max comments to Sophie about how quiet the office is compared to others in which Max has worked. Several times during the morning too Max has observed Sophie emailing a colleague sitting just two desks away. "No one ever to talks to anyone anymore. Is this always the case or is this just today?" Max asks Sophie.

"I often feel it would be quicker to go and talk to someone but email is the norm in this office. In my previous office there was much more of a buzz. Sometimes when an email discussion was getting out of hand the owner of the discussion would call a quick ten-minute chat to resolve things. We even had a few fun activities such as no email afternoons and no emails within a five desk radius. But here everyone just relies on email," says Sophie looking a little downcast.

Max says, "It is interesting that often even in restaurants and at social gatherings people often have their heads in their mobile device rather than enjoying the here and now of their present company. So little wonder new joiners bring what they see as acceptable behaviour to the office."

Max poses two questions to Sophie: "Is it right to be so reliant on email?" and "What are the alternatives and when is it best to use them?"

"Until now I have worked using my instinct having no guidelines to follow," says Sophie. "Are there any you can suggest?" she asks batting the ball back into Max's court.

Why bother to look outside the inbox?

By nature Sophie is a bubbly outgoing person who loves talking but often also does it through text and other instant messaging applications such as 'WhatsApp'. As they talk through this email fixation (come addiction) Sophie admits that she misses talking to people because she feels she has a blinkered view of what is happening.

"You are right," Max replies. "With email you have no way to convey feelings, either yours or the recipient's. Yet, email is just one of a huge and ever growing way to communicate. Used incorrectly, it's like using a sledgehammer to crack open a nut. An email sent in haste can mean you pour cold water onto someone's great idea, which might have helped you develop a relationship, even a new stream of business.

Other things Max suggests thinking about include:

- What sitting hunched over either a laptop or mobile device is doing to your wellbeing as discussed in the next chapter.

- The lack of body language. Email can damage relationships and professional image. In haste we often say things that are either best left unsaid or if spoken would be toned down when we see the other person's body language. For example, the word 'thanks' could be interpreted as either a genuine complement or sarcasm.
- The number of rounds of fruitless email ping-pong needed to reach a decision. The result can be either the wrong or even no decision. Both instances are bad for you and your business and it may not be possible to retrieve the situation.
- Sending ten people a large attachment that only one person really needs. This too is a quick way to spoil good relationships and hack off your colleagues (even clients).

All these downsides of an email-centric culture contribute to poor performance, not only in the sense of email overload but also in terms of poor communication and reduced well-being. All are largely intertwined.

"So what are my options given that many people stick to email and are reluctant to step outside the inbox?" Sophie asks Max.

Email's fatal attraction

"First," Max replies, "you need to ask why business people are so attached to email, at least those who are over 30 years old. Then we can start looking at guidelines for using alternative ways to communicate more efficiently and effectively, and how to coax others to change their email behaviour. In most cases the attraction to email is related to one of six main reasons or a combination of them."

Why are we addicted to email?

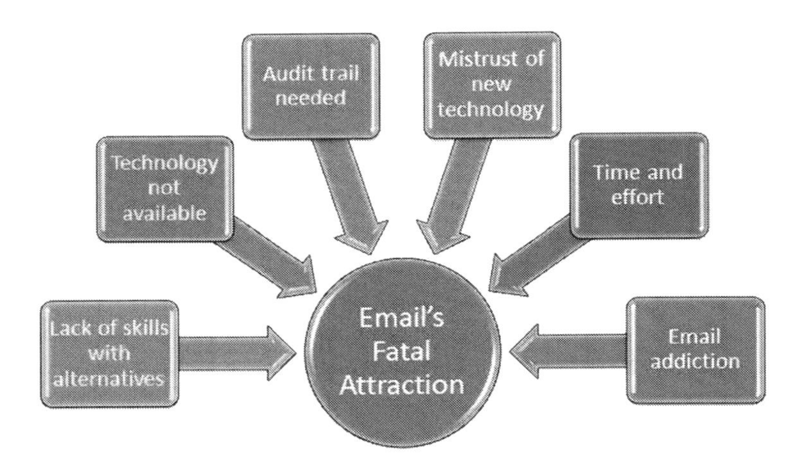

An audit trail is needed (or perceived as necessary), which can be hard with a conversation. Hence all the Cc'd emails.

- Lack of skills and knowledge to use alternative media such as collaborative tools like SharePoint, OneNote, etc. They are not intuitive and can be hard to use for those with limited IT skills.
- Mistrust of alternative technologies such as instant messaging – for example, it's easy either to bully or feel bullied through instant messaging. People can use it to attract your attention even though you are busy.

- Time and effort. It might take longer to talk but the outcome will be better. However that is a balancing act.
- **Email addiction. This is a real disease of 21st century business life:** the feeling that you cannot survive without a quick fix of email every few minutes. Even just checking and seeing no new emails is a sufficient fix for the email addict.

"It's little wonder then that we often revert to email when in reality an alternative would be much more effective, from talking via IM to even pen and paper," voices Max.

To email or not to email

I like to listen. I have learned a great deal from listening carefully. Most people never listen.

Ernest Hemingway

Range of communications channels

Max suggests that if we look at the alternatives we can then try to draw out some options and guidelines. The alternatives to email are many and varied and in most offices include those over the page.

Alternatives to email

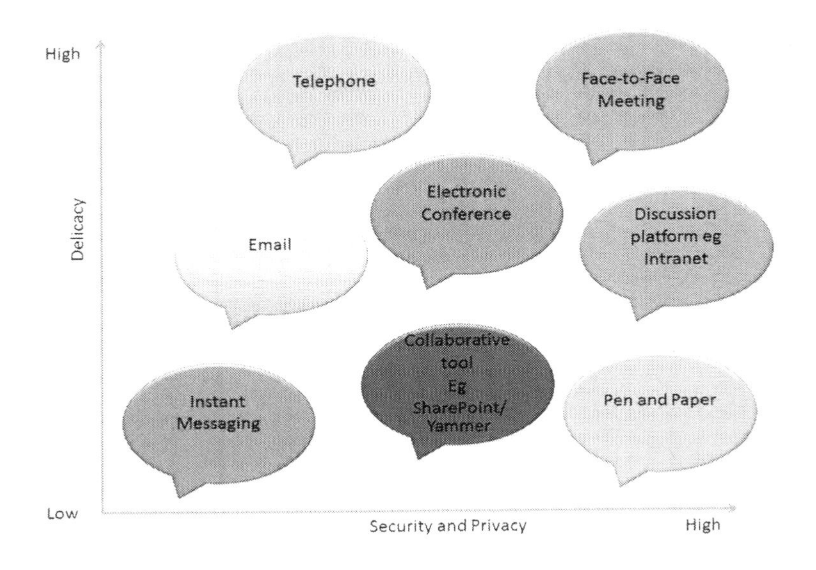

The degree of privacy and delicacy each communication channel offers varies as does the ability to see and gauge the other person's behaviour and emotions. Text messaging, for example, is open but lacks any way of showing feelings, whereas a face-to-face meeting (real or virtual) is rich in context and ability to see behavioural and emotional language.

Socially these days, many feel it is acceptable to share their every thought and move through social media platforms such as Facebook and WhatsApp. In business a level of security and privacy is still important. That must not be confused with mistrust and lack of transparency, which are quite different matters.

For example, **mistrust might be a reason why everyone copies in everyone else: they are covering their backside in case anyone lays the blame at their door.** Being opaque might equate to when people use their private email account for business matters in order to hide something: this is not untypical in the public sector and is the source of many an email scandal (including Michael Gove in 2012 and Hilary Clinton in 2015).

PNPD framework for choosing the medium

In the business context, there are four factors to consider when choosing an alternative communications channel. Max calls this his **'PNPD framework'.**

- Privacy – what level of privacy is needed?
- Numbers – is it one-to-one or one-to-many?
- Permanency – do you need an audit trail of the exchange?
- Delicacy – how important is it to be able to see the other person's reaction as you converse so as to moderate what you say accordingly?

Here are a few examples to illustrate the PNPD principle for a variety of communications.

Scenario 1 – Conversation

Private between two people, delicate but a permanent record of the final discussion will be needed (for example, performance appraisal, salary negotiation, disciplinary meeting).

Best option – conversation (face-to-face if possible otherwise virtual) followed up by an email confirming the discussion.

Privacy is high; Numbers are low; Permanency is high; Delicacy is high.

Scenario 2 – Instant messaging

A public message for several people if not the whole office, which if not seen here and now is of no relevance later. It does not matter how people react. For example, testing the fire alarm, cakes for your birthday.

Best option – Instant messaging.

Privacy is low; Numbers are high; Permanency is low; Delicacy is low.

Scenario 3 – Email

A message for several people, which they need to see and for which evidence of its distribution is needed (that is, a permanent record is required) and for which recipients' reactions do not matter. For example, change in contract details, cover for leave, new fees, delivery of materials on-site. If the message is internal it is hoped that privacy is maintained. For external use, steps maybe needed to manage any breach of confidentiality and this is discussed in Chapter 14.

Best option – Email.

Privacy is medium; Numbers are medium; Permanency is high; Delicacy is low.

Scenario 4 – Collaborative tools (for example, SharePoint, Yammer, Slack etc.)

Several of you are working on the same project and need to share files and other information. Files are medium size (between 2 and 3MB) and frequently updated. Members of the team are not always in the office, some work from home and some on-site. Privacy is important as the files contain confidential information, but how people react to the information is not that important in terms of emotions.

Best option – Collaborative tools such as SharePoint, OneNote etc. with access limited only to team members.

Privacy is high; Numbers are medium; Permanency is high; Delicacy is low.

Scenario 5 – Pen and paper

A colleague has gone the extra mile to help you, saving you time and reducing the risk of making a gaff. You want to thank them. You want to make them smile and realise just how much you appreciate their help.

Best option – a card/hand written note to say thank you.

Privacy is medium; Numbers are low; Permanency is high; Delicacy is high.

As you can see, choosing an alternative to email is not always straightforward explains Max. Generally the two key factors are the delicacy of the communication (and especially how important it is to see the other person's reactions as you communicate) and the number of people involved. Here is a summary using these two criteria.

PNPD framework for thinking outside the inbox

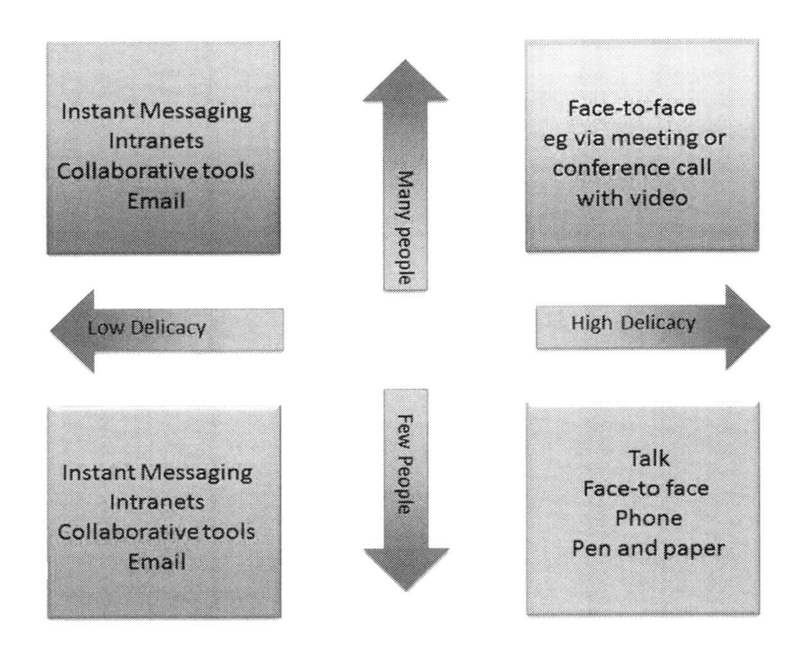

Seven top ways to think outside the inbox

We must adjust to changing times
and still hold to unchanging principles.

Jimmy Carter

In addition to the PNDP principles Max offers seven golden ground rules to help decide when stepping outside the inbox might be more productive.

1. *Call me if it's urgent.* Never assume that the other person is checking each new email as it arrives. Most people respond the quickest to a phone call or even a text message. If the other person is in the office, walk and talk for anything very urgent.

2. *Use collaborative tools to share material and especially files* rather than sending each person an email. The main benefits are that everyone has the current information and people's inboxes are not being fattened up with large and often unnecessary attachments.

Some organisations have very successfully banned all internal email and replaced it with internal social media platforms designed specifically for their own use. These include Atos, the French technology company, and a UK Housing Association. They report increased performance and a 64 percent reduction in email traffic.

3. *Talk first email later.* Whenever something is delicate and/or confidential, always talk before sending an email. It is very easy to take words in an email out of context and unintentionally start an email war. Furthermore, an email is about as secure and confidential as a postcard. Send it to the wrong person and 'pow' it's gone viral before you can blink.

This way you have a chance to navigate the conversation depending on the other person's facial and body language.

4. *Ban emails within a five desk radius* and, wherever possible, go and talk to the person. Again, you will be fitter and might be very surprised at how much additional information you pick up on the way, for example, new job and sales opportunities, fresh research data, or the chance to get to know a new or existing colleague better. It can also help you improve your personal wellbeing by ensuring you walk more and sit less.

5. *Use instant messaging* for broadcast messages that have low privacy and a short shelf-life. It's quick and easy and means people don't waste time deleting/replying to unnecessary emails.

6. *Make your own reminder when someone asks you to do something.* Don't reply by saying – "email me". Take ownership and write it down for yourself (on paper or electronically). Despite being in a so-called electronic age and, for some, a paperless office, it is surprising how many people still carry around a conventional note book (either traditional paper or electronic such as OneNote). The exception is when you are driving: even with hands-free phones there is evidence to show that you have reduced your ability to concentrate on the road.

7. *Stop playing email ping-pong after round five.* If an email exchange is not moving forward, stop and talk. If necessary call an impromptu meeting to resolve the matter (face-to-face or virtual according to the geographic location of those involved).

From this you will gather that despite being a person of the 21st Century Max is still very much a believer in talking as one of the most effective ways to communicate.

An email sent is an email retained for life

Despite all you hear and read, it is a myth that you can delete emails you wish you had never sent. You might well delete the offending email and send a follow-up apology. Your organisation may have a process for deleting all emails over 90 days old – not uncommon in the public sector.

However the recipient, over whom you have no control, may well have kept a copy! Moreover some organisations archive every email sent and received for audit purposes (e-disclosure) and especially those governed by US laws.

Bad emails turn up just like the proverbial bad penny and can be very damaging just as the likes of Sony, News International and many others have discovered to their dismay. Socially, many of the younger generation (Z and Millennials) have shunned email and turned to alternative platforms which self-destruct after a message is read (for example, Snapchat and Slack). While this is fine for social interactions, it is really not an option for business.

The moral is *think before hitting send* and ask yourself *what would happen if your email was found by the wrong person*? If you have doubts don't send it. Find an alternative way to communicate – if you must say anything.

Fine but… How to help others think outside the inbox

If you are given a chance to be a role model, I think you should always take it because you can influence a person's life in a positive light, and that's what I want to do. That's what it's all about.

Tiger Woods

"This is all good common sense," says Sophie feeling as though she has just attended a university lecture about electronic communications. "How can I go against the prevailing email-centric culture?" she asks Max.

"Granted, it is not easy and you cannot change behaviour let alone organisational culture overnight. Indeed it has been said that it takes between 21 and 66 days to form a new habit. For a golfer they often need to hit about 10,000 balls before they ingrain a new swing change," Max replies.

"Nonetheless Sophie, as one of the organisation's most respected Assistants, you can start by setting the leadership model. Your behaviour and attitude will influence that of others often. This is often referred to as the Bataris Box," explains Max to a worried looking Sophie.

Bataris box for influencing behaviour

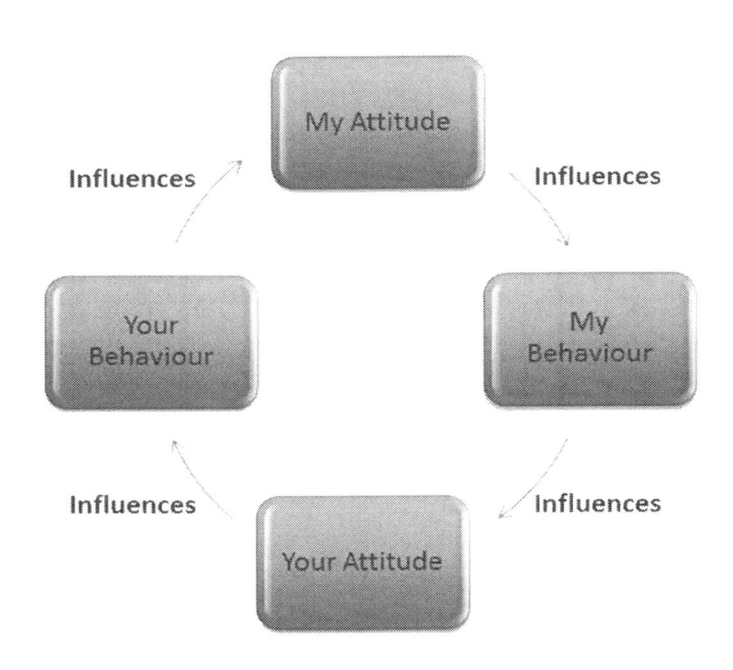

"As you start to step outside the inbox and choose to use alternatives, so others will start to follow," he adds. Here are some ways that others have used successfully.

The Whiteboard

A defence company installed whiteboards in strategic places across the department and then banned all ephemeral social emails and told people to use the white boards for the messages instead. For example, cakes for my birthday, printer 1 is down, has anyone seem my Cherries mug, fire alarm being tested at 2.00 pm, etc. This was a great success and people loved walking down the office to see what was happening in other parts.

No email within a five desk radius

If you break the ban unnecessarily there is a small fine (for instances donation to the charity of the month/year).

First one to check their mobile device over a meal pays the bill – several colleagues

That soon stops people checking unless there is a really water tight reason – for example, someone is ill.

Make it worthwhile to talk to me

Offer a reward – for example, chocolate/fruit nuts etc. People soon start to come and see you instead of replying by email.

Email free periods

Companies set aside a specific time (Friday pm) when all internal emails are answered by conversation either phone or walk and talk. Some still have these periods; others use them from time to time to remind colleagues that there is life outside the inbox.

Keep my calendar clear

Email traffic was building up because everyone was constantly in meetings. The top management team at a top 10 university decided to have 'meeting free Fridays' whenever possible. That way people knew their director would be available. The volume of email traffic quickly went down.

Thank-you cards

Virgin keep a store of fun thank-you cards, which they send to someone when they have really exceeded expectation. Sometimes the card includes a bar of chocolate. These expressions of gratitude are always much appreciated by the recipient and almost become a badge of honour.

Phone call to relay highly sensitive information

One of the major private insurance companies always telephones to discuss their response to a request to cover a medical procedure. Most claims are dealt with immediately when the person phones, but for some complex situations the request is referred to a specialist team. While supporting papers can be emailed to the company, they will never email their response. This is to ensure confidentiality and the highest level of security.

Max suggests Sophie try one or two of these options over the next few months and especially the email free time, thank-you cards and no emails within a five desk radius.

Then they sift through some of the new emails – there are three from David Butler. Plucking up courage, she walks up a floor to find the sender and deal with his requests. *En route* Sophie finds herself invited to a review of a new product (there have been a few cancellations at tomorrow's launch), and hears that another colleague is moving departments.

Within five minutes Sophie has dealt with all three emails from David, and she has strengthened their working relationship as she was able to impart information related to another relevant project (and which he might not have found out about until it was too late). Thinking outside the inbox becomes a win-win situation in the long term.

Summary

- Many people are addicted to email and is one reason why they rely solely on it.
- Think before hitting send. Email is just one of many ways to communicate. Depending on the Privacy, Number of People involved, Permanency and Delicacy of the message, an alternative is often more effective.
- Talking can often be as effective as email as it saves time and reduces the risk of misinterpretation and igniting an email war.
- When the message is confidential or delicate (that is, it's important to see the other person's reaction), talk first and email later.

- For ephemeral messages with a very short shelf-life and for which no record is needed, more effective options include instant messaging and writing them on a whiteboard.
- To share information with several people, collaborative tools are better – for example, SharePoint, intranet discussion boards, OneNote etc.
- Pen and paper still has a place for showing appreciation, taking ownership and making a reminder to yourself when asked to do something.
- Thinking outside the inbox and using alternatives will influence other people's email behaviour and encourage them too to think and act outside the inbox.

8

Are you sitting comfortably?

I want to get old gracefully. I want to have good posture, I want to be healthy and be an example to my children.

Sting

How does spending too long dealing with email affect our well-being?

There have been several studies over the past decade, which link the rise in musculoskeletal disease to the increased time we spend working at our computers. In 2013 it was estimated that in the **UK businesses lost about 30 million days through musculoskeletal related illness such as chronic back, lower limb and wrist and hand problems.**

In 2014, the British Chiropractic Society found that the prevalence of back and neck pain has increased by ten percent over the past year across all age groups. They found that on average we now spend about ten hours sitting down and less than two hours being active. The first sign of today's sedentary work life is stress. But the underpinning cause of the stress is often muscle tension. Many people look more like their cave men ancestors than their parents.

Max says, "The prevalence of back pain was brought home to me when a young friend said they needed to see an osteopath because of reading their emails on their laptop while sitting on an office sofa. Suffice to say the employer is paying for their back treatment." Max has also noted a rise in the number of people having treatment for repetitive strain injuries (RSI) to their wrist and hand resulting from continuous use of a keyboard and poor posture at the desk.

'Text neck' is a phrase coined recently to describe the neck pain many suffer as a result of the neck disorders caused by hanging the head while using a mobile devise (be it to text, email, post on social media, etc). The average head weighs 10 pounds. Every inch you tilt it forward to read a mobile device adds more pressure to your spine. When your ears drop over your shoulders it makes your head feel more like 20 to 30 pounds.

Eyes too become strained and fatigued with prolonged looking at a screen, which can result in headaches and deteriorating vision. Look at how many people now wear glasses (and not simply as a fashion accessory). Common eye aliments now include itchy, watery and dry eye syndrome. Eye strain is so prevalent that it is now classed as a form of RSI.

Max says to Sophie that he has seen her several times slumped over her laptop and iPad. Yet when they have walked out for a coffee she has a model's classic upright stance and could easily have balanced a book on her head if asked.

Well-being is a key value for many organisations and certainly for Sophie. Indeed her executive Richard is one of the well-being principal sponsors and she is a well-being champion.

"Yes," interjects Sophie. "I too have been to an osteopath a couple of times in the past few months and last year had treatment for *De Quervain's* tenosynovitis. The tendons linking my thumb and wrist were so inflamed they had to be injected with cortisone. It was painful and tedious as I could not use my right hand for 48 hours after the treatment and even then had to take great care and wear a splint for a month."

Max suggests that **adopting a good computer and desk posture can help Sophie save time dealing with her email, because it will improve her overall well-being** and hence enable her to be more alert and productive.

Sophie asks Max if they can digress for a few minutes from the actual inbox management to run through a checklist of key posture-related tips. "That's just what I was going to suggest," replies Max. "Here are my top tips drawn from talking to the medical experts (such as physiotherapists, back surgeons, orthopaedic specialists, ophthalmic consultants, osteopaths, fitness coaches and GPs etc)."

Overall well-being

The crux is to think 20 and take regular breaks. Our body can only tolerate being in the same position for 20 to 30 minutes maximum before tension starts to creep in (this applies for all devices).

Here are six ways to stay energised and keep your muscles as relaxed as possible. These apply no matter what device you are using:

- Stop frequently and do some stretching and breathing exercise for two minutes (for example, back, neck, hands, even legs). Even take a quick walk. It is all too easy for our lungs to be restricted when sitting hunched up. This means that insufficient oxygen reaches our body and it slows our metabolism. Hence we start to feel sluggish and that is when errors happen: emails are sent in haste when 'slow email' would have been better and prevented an email disaster come war.
- The optimum 20 minutes might be hard, but at least aim for a two-minute break every hour.
- Eat your lunch away from your desk. It is amazing what you find in people's keyboards. The keyboard and mouse are also harbingers of bacteria. So this is about hygiene too.
- Keep hydrated. We often become either so engrossed in our work or distracted by new emails and social media alerts that it is easy to forget to drink water. Ideally you should drink about 1.5 litres of water per day. That can be hard so set a sensible goal of say .75 litres.
- Eat healthy food like fruit and health bars. Chocolate in moderation is a good source of energy but you may find yourself on a roller coaster – enjoying a sugar rush but then a crash as the effects wear off. Avoid too much junk food.
- **Switch off all technology devices at least one hour before going to sleep.** Computer screens have been found to disturb sleep patterns as they affect our melatonin levels, which in turn affect our circadian rhythm.

Sophie says that she does try to eat as healthily as possible, and goes to the gym and practices yoga regularly. But she had not thought of using some of the stretching exercise she does at the gym in the office in small doses. Max says she might be surprised at how many top executives these days try to find time to practice some yoga and mindfulness techniques during the day just to stay focused and calm.

Posture

People don't realize that when they 'throw out' their back, it's often because of weak abs. These muscles are essential for lower-back strength and good posture.

Sylvester Stallone

Max explains that the key to good posture is to think right angles (90^0) for your knees, elbows and hips. These should be open at just over 90^0. Here are seven ways to reduce straining your neck, head, arm and wrist:

1. Sit up straight and support your back properly. Use your chair back rest to help you. Avoid slumping over the keyboard like James in this picture.

Poor posture

Why? If you look more closely you will see:

- Core – the abdominals are collapsed, all the weight is forwards forcing the ribs and the chest forwards.
- Shoulders and arms – the keyboard is way forward and the arms and shoulders follow.
- Neck – possibly the worse part, the neck has to extend back in order to view the screen.

2. Sit at the right height. Your arms should form an L shape with the forearms resting vertically on the keyboard. Avoid sitting either too low or too high as this too encourages you to tilt forward and slouch.

3. Keep your feet flat on the floor. Use a foot rest if needed and especially if you are short and your feet don't touch

the floor. Avoid either tucking them under your chair, or lowering the chair (as this can cause muscle tension on the arms). A proper position helps your back and stops muscle tension in the ankles.

4. **Set the monitor at the right height – eye level.** The top of the screen (monitor) should be just level with your eyes (for a 15 to 17 inch one). Too low and you will be slouching as you move away from the chair to see the screen and putting undue strain on your neck muscles. To some extent 'eye level' also depends on how you type.

If you touch type try raising the monitor so the top section is just visible below eye level. If you 'hunt and peck' and need to see the keyboard, try having the monitor a fraction lower to reduce unnecessary raising and lowering of the head.

5. Place the screen at an arm's length away from you.

6. Keep the keyboard and mouse close to hand. Ideally your keyboard should be four to six inches from the front of the desk to allow your wrists to be properly supported. Stretching each time for the mouse will put undue strain on your shoulder muscles and spine. If you use a laptop for an extended period consider using a mouse rather than the touch pad.

7. De-clutter your desk and make it easy to access anything else you frequently use – for example, the phone. Again repeated stretching to reach the phone and papers, etc., will put a strain on your back and shoulder muscles.

"Using these guidelines, let's re-look at James," says Max.

Good posture

We now see:

- Core – slightly engaged. The trunk is more upright.
- Shoulders and arms – are in the back one third of the body.
- Neck – crown lifting up towards the ceiling.

Eye care

Keep your eyes on the stars, and your feet on the ground.

Theodore Roosevelt

We forget, says Max, what a strain looking at a screen of any size puts on our eyes. For instance, **squinting puts a strain on the eye muscles and should be avoided wherever possible**. Even if you have 20/20 vision you must protect it by reducing the need to screw up your eyes to read the screen (whether because either the font is too small or the light is poor). Here are the key essential ways the medical profession suggest we can reduce the wear and tear on our eyes. Again the key is to think 20.

1. Take regular breaks and refocus your eyes every 20 to 30 minutes. Look away from the screen for a few seconds and focus on something else and preferably a distant object, which is at least 20 feet away. This reduces the risk of your eyes getting locked on one focal range (for example, near vision). Studies in the US found that after prolonged periods at the computer, speed and accuracy declines. After a break, however, both improve again.
2. Blink often as this helps moisten the eyes and reduces dryness and tiredness.
3. Adjust the screen brightness, background colour and font size to suit you. For example, if you are working in a poorly lit area (for example, on a client site), increase the screen's brightness. Conversely dim the screen if you are working in a well-lit area. Zoom in on pages (of files and websites) if they are too small to read comfortably. For inputting text, 12-point font is the best. Much smaller and you will be squinting. If the company policy is to use a smaller font, then increase it artificially by using the zoom function.

4. Read long articles offline and on paper. Reading on the screen can be very tiring.

Mobile devices

On the one hand, Max suggests mobile devices afford the opportunity to stand up. On the other hand, however, they can be more harmful than proper computers because they are so small and addictive. 'IPad Neck' is the phrase used by many to describe the sore neck and back many users suffer. Again the key is good posture and regular breaks. The best practice outlined for the eyes and postures in general apply equally for using a mobile device. In addition the current advice is:

1. **Keep upright (standing or sitting) and hold the device vertically and at face level rather than bending over it.**
2. Don't grip it too tightly for too long. Again this will help relax the hand and arm muscles, which will otherwise become tense.
3. Prop up the device – for example, have a cover that can double as a stand or a proper mobile device holder.
4. When using the device as a phone, avoid wedging it between your shoulders and face to talk. Hold it to your ear, alternatively use either headphones with a built-in microphone or the built-in speaker. Again, this will reduce the strain on the back and neck muscles.
5. Reducing the stress on your thumbs is hard (often called Blackberry Thumb). Try not to stab at the keys. Press them lightly. Otherwise for prolonged use either attach a small keyboard or use a stylus.

Max says that most experts agree that finding ways to use mobile devices properly for long periods of time is quite hard just because of their very tactile nature. We often want to keep them handy and grab them when sitting (and lying down). Taking a break and even disconnecting is also an important way to reduce the risk of long-term damage to our body and especially neck, shoulders and back. There are also some apps available that prompt you to take a break and give advice on good posture – and, hence, reduce the ergonomic risks associated with prolonged mobile device usage.

"Now that sounds interesting," says Sophie, making a note to look these up and at least try them on her personal mobile device. If she finds one she likes she can then request it for the work ones.

Sophie comments that they are also having a well-being week soon. Whilst there will be keep fit, yoga and mindfulness taster sessions, these tips will make useful reminders for us to post on the internal social media discussion boards.

"Let's practice what we have discussed," Max says to Sophie. "Time for a break."

Summary

- Good posture and eye care is essential to maintaining one's well-being as it limits the risk of muscle tension and hence the associated musculoskeletal disease, which affects so many people in today's digital world.
- Think 20. Take a break from the computer every 20 minutes or so and at the most every hour. Use your lunch time as one of the breaks and avoid eating at your desk.

- Stretch your muscles and re-focus your eyes during the breaks.
- Maintain a good posture regardless of the device you are using. Avoid hunching over the keyboard and slouching in your chair.
- Ensure your keyboard and mouse are close to hand and that your arms form an L when using them.
- Set the top of your monitor at eye level and at arm's length from you.
- Keep hydrated and try to eat healthily.
- Switch off all devices at least one hour before going to sleep.
- Hold mobile devices and especially the phone at face level rather than hunching over it. With the phone desist from wedging it between your face and neck. Hold it to your ear or, alternatively, use either the speaker or headphones.
- Reduce the tendency to stab at the screen of a mobile device. Experiment with mobile keyboards and/or a stylus.
- When using a mobile device for extended periods try an app to help you manage your time and limit the associated ergonomic risks associated with it such as iPad and text neck.

9

Email etiquette – why bother?

Whatever words we utter should be chosen with care for people will hear them and be influenced by them for good or ill.

Buddha

Throughout the day, Max carefully observes how Sophie writes her emails. In some cases he notices she responds in haste often with just one or two words such as "OK", "Thanks" and "That's good". At other times she writes long emails almost like a brain dump.

Greetings range from nothing to a simple "Hi" and on occasion the person's name. Sign offs are similarly inconsistent too, sometimes just a smiley and less frequently a more formal closure such as "kind regards".

As to subject lines, she always replies using the one the sender used. When she writes a new email, the subject line generally consists of one or at most three words – for example, meeting, a quotation, flights, etc. From time to time, Max watches Sophie trawl her sent items and re-send certain emails asking if the person has had time to read her original email. This seems frequently to be when the original was long and rambling. From time to time she adds a High Priority marker to the follow-up.

Over their break, Max suggests that they talk about Sophie's choice of greetings, and the way she's worded the content and then signed off her emails. At first Sophie is a little indignant because she sees herself as a digital native, having grown up with social media apps such as Facebook, Instagram and WhatsApp. She has the feeling that Max, while very well educated and experienced in business, is more of a digital newcomer. Max, she knows, has agreed email is an integral part of business communications, but social media only came into being half way through Max's career. So she challenges Max, asking:

"What's the problem? It should be intuitive and I have been using email and apps such as WhatsApp almost since I was able to walk! I had my first iPad when I was five."

Your digital dress code

Focusing isn't just an optical activity, it is also a mental one

Bridget Riley

"That's not the issue," says Max emphatically. "The issue is what impression your email gives of you and your company. When I read your email, I form an impression of you within three seconds and, consequently, whether or not I really want to work with you. There may be no choice, but if it's a customer relationship, I can take my business elsewhere."

Max settles down to explain that during his years as CEO of a large international hi-tech company, one of the most difficult things to get right was the fine line between what was acceptable digital etiquette for social e-communications (for example, email and social media) and what works best in business. "Socially you generally know the person who you are connected with (for example, on WhatsApp). Also rarely, if ever, do you need a permanent record (audit trail) of your communications – for example, as evidence in the event of a court case. In business, however, you might find your emails being used as evidence. Worse still, if the business email system is hacked, your emails may end up on the front page of the national press and social media and can be very damaging."

Max cites two prime examples of where emails have damaged reputation: Barclays Bank emails at the height of the Libor scandal (2012) and, more recently, emails that came out when Sony was hacked in 2014. Abusive and arrogant emails from the then CEO (Amy Pascal) were found and leaked to the press by the hackers. She subsequently stepped down. In Barclays' case very exuberant gung-ho emails emerged about how traders communicated with each other both to manipulate the exchange rates and then express appreciation for the deals. Barclays CEO (Bob Diamond) was fired and the bank's reputation was severely damaged.

In business you may never have met the person with whom you are corresponding (be they internal or external). Your email is therefore your 'digital dress code'. It creates an impression of you. When you walk into a room of people you don't know, whether to network or for a job interview, you need to create a positive professional image so that you stand out. The same applies for email. The recipient, like you, may have 50-plus emails a day.

Max tells Sophie, "To get your emails read you need to **consider how you can make your email stand out in a crowded inbox, not in an arrogant pushy way, but subtly** so that your recipients notice it and feel drawn to respond. If you can address this, it will also help reduce the number of times you need to send a follow-up to prompt a response."

"Sophie, we have spent almost a day together," Max adds. "And I can see that you are an intelligent, charming, well organised and very highly regarded member of the organisation. So let me show you how to use email etiquette to your advantage to convey these qualities and ensure your emails are read and answered properly."

Excellent emails – five key elements

Below are the five key elements of an excellent email designed to grab the recipient's attention.

Five elements of excellent emails

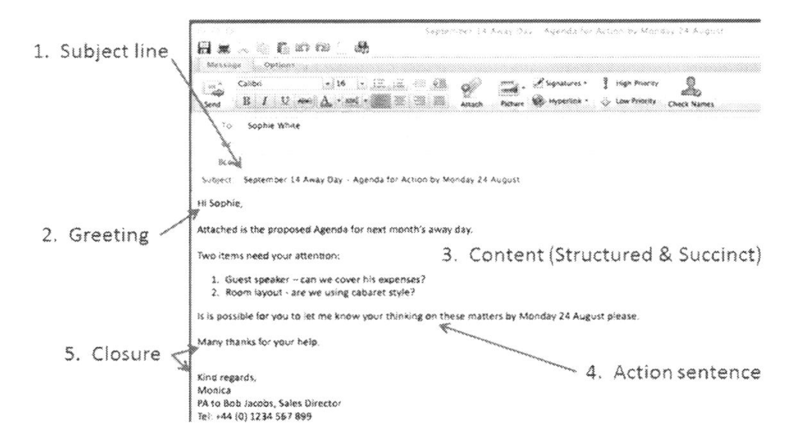

Over the next three chapters we will look at these in more detail.

10

Gaining attention – subject lines, address box and greetings

Marketing is a contest for people's attention.

Seth Godin

Max suggests to Sophie that they now look in more detail at how excellent email etiquette can help her not only gain the recipient's attention, but also maintain it, so they read to the end and respond to all her questions.

The good subject line

People often boast about how many unread emails are in their main inbox – not the sub-folders, just the actual top level inbox folder. In many cases this can be several thousand. To compete for attention amid all of this communication is simple, says Max: '**The subject line is your opening gambit. It's like walking into a crowded room.** Your subject line must make your email stand out in the recipient's inbox, which is probably already full."

Here are the three key elements of a good subject-line:

1. Precisely and accurately reflects the content.
2. Includes the date by when action is required (if appropriate).
3. Indicates the purpose of the email (for example, for action or information only).

Examples are:

- Board Meeting on 12 July – details of location and travel arrangements. Respond by 1 July
- June 2015 milk sales figures – FYI
- Conference call Monday 12 August at 2.30 log in details - FYI

In each case the subject line is precise rather than vague, such as, Board Meeting, Sales Figures and Conference Call.

Subject line faux pas

This is why a good subject line is so important Max emphasises to Sophie. "So what should I avoid?" Sophie asks. Max outlines two basic but common mistakes:

- No subject line.
- A subject line that bears no relationship to the content of the email. This often happens when either you use an old email to start a new conversation or you continue with an existing email but change topics. In this instance either start a completely fresh email or at the very least

change the subject line to reflect a change in direction of the conversation.

In both these cases you reduce the chance of your email being seen and give the appearance of being sloppy.

Say it in the subject line

If your email is very short, you can save time – for you and the recipient, by saying what you have to say in the subject line alone and end it with the abbreviation EOM standing for End of Message. For example:

June 2015 Sales for Zurich attached – EOM
Meeting room changed to Room 101 – EOM
July 2015 Board Meeting draft minutes attached – EOM

In each case this implies that you have nothing else to say and hence do not need to waste time greeting the recipient and composing a succinct message, which in all likelihood will duplicate the subject line. It also implies that no reply is needed from the recipient.

With Max's help Sophie uses this for a couple of her one-line emails and is pleasantly surprised at the time she saves and the fact it helps further to reduce the email traffic.

"OK," says Max. "Now you have successfully gained the recipient's attention as you walk into their inbox, you now need to find ways to maintain it so they want to read on and develop a business relationship as appropriate. They need to have a virtual image of you as professional, well organised and making a contribution to their busy lives. Email is two way, it's not just about you wanting information and telling people things. The other person needs to feel there is something in it for them in reading your email. You need to make it easy for them, because they are as time poor as you."

To Cc or Bcc... Which is correct?

Max notices that in addition to reading the emails addressed direct to Sophie, she also meticulously reads, and sometimes replies to, those in which she is Cc'd. Max quizzes Sophie about this: surely this is wasting time because only those emails where she is in the 'To' box require action – that is, reading and/or replying?

"Oh I wish," says Sophie. "For me Cc means carbon copy – for information only. But often people include me in the Cc box and expect me to action some aspect of the email! Suggestions please?" she asks Max looking troubled.

"You are of course right," Max replies. "It's difficult if not everyone adopts the correct email etiquette about the address line. First, let's lay down the correct email etiquette rules for these three address lines. These will gain you respect from colleagues."

Address line	Purpose
To	For me and it requires some form of action. That may be to perform a task and respond accordingly, for example, to arrange a meeting, obtain data, create a presentation, etc. Alternatively it can just mean, read and take note of what I am saying, but no direct response is expected.
Cc	Copied for information only. You are not expected to respond unless you spot something is very wrong. In that instance, the etiquette is to *reply only to the sender*, unless the sender asks for a 'Reply All'. *To Reply All is considered politically incorrect and looks like you are trying to score points over the sender.*
Bcc	This should only be used when sending one email to multiple people. It reduces the risk of a Reply All and improves confidentiality, because each person can only see their own name. One client sent one email to all the third party re-sellers using the Cc box. You can imagine the uproar when A discovered that B was also a re-seller! Putting all the names in the Bcc box avoids making such an email blunder. If you do need to send a conventional blind copy to keep them in the loop, the correct email etiquette is to forward the original email and tell them why you are blind copying them in.

"Well I know that, it was drilled into us at Business School," says Sophie. "But what about those who don't and persist in misusing the address line and using the Cc box like a safety net to make sure they have told everyone?"

"They are the difficult players," says Max. "But take heart. There are a few things you can do to change people's behaviour and help them see the errors of their email behaviour. Here are a few of them."

- Use the right box yourself.
- Avoid confusion. **Where you include several people in the 'To' line, be explicit about what you expect from each individual** – for example, A to arrange travel, B the meeting papers, etc.
- Reduce the number of people you, as a sender, include in the Cc box.
- Avoid using 'Reply All' unless specifically asked to use it by the sender.
- If you are in the Cc line and action is expected, gently point out the error of the sender's way and suggest that in future they use the 'To' box. Indeed many people that Max works with now receive so much Cc'd email, that they filter it out on arrival using rules. Then they see only what is a real priority for them.
- If you are in the 'To' box with multiple other people, reply to the sender asking what is expected of you personally.

Changing behaviour is not easy as we discussed earlier. The best you can do is lead by example and gain the respect of those with whom you work most closely. Sooner or later they will be fed up with your questions, and getting no response when you are in the Cc line will start to adopt your principles. You know what they say – if you can't beat them, join them!

Greet me with respect

Email is very informal, a memo. But I find that not signing off or not having a salutation bothers me.

Judith Martin

Max says that research shows that the simple act of greeting the other person is like a handshake and draws them one more step into your world. No greeting, meanwhile, creates an impression of arrogance – that you are too busy to focus on anyone else. The greeting, however, must be professional. Suggested examples include:

- Person's name
- Dear
- Good morning, afternoon etc.
- Hi
- Hello

The last two are less formal and more appropriate for people you know quite well. "If you are responding to an email and especially from someone you don't know particularly well, then mirror their greeting," adds Max.

"But what if it either doesn't contain a greeting or, worse, has an inappropriate greeting?" asks Sophie. "I have had emails where the sender addresses me as 'Hi Doll' or 'Alright Sophie'."

"In such situations **reply along the same line of informality but just notch it up a level or two.** For example, using "Hi", "Hello" or their name. While still informal, it conveys the professional approach and, at the same time, says we are not friends but rather business colleagues," says Max. "That way you are, again, setting the role model for email best practice (just as we discussed earlier)."

Max says that in a business context, attention to small matters such as how you greet other people all add to the bigger picture of a caring person who wants to build relationships. After all, you wouldn't just walk up to a person and start babbling, so why do it with an email?

Summary

- Use the correct address line: 'To' is for action, 'Cc' is for information only and 'Bcc' is best reserved for sending one email to multiple people.
- If you need to blind copy in another person, forward the original with a note about why.
- Avoid 'Reply All' like the plague.
- Always include an accurate subject line, which reflects the content of the email.
- Insert an indication of the purpose of your email – for example, for action and by when, information only, etc.
- Say it in the subject line for very short emails where you are conveying information and no response is needed – for example, change of location.
- When the original email contains no subject line – add one.
- When the content of the email conversation changes, modify the subject line accordingly.

- Always greet the recipient using a professional greeting such as Dear, Hi and their name.
- If they fail to include a greeting, make sure you respond with one.
- If you feel the greeting is inappropriate, respond with an appropriate one.

11

Maintaining attention – the content

Music is powered by ideas. If you don't have clarity of ideas, you're just communicating sheer sound.

Yo-Yo Ma

From time to time, Max notices that Sophie opens an email, glances at it and then closes it. "What is that about?" Max enquires.

"In some way the content has annoyed me," replies Sophie.

Max probes, asking, "In what way? Was it the length (some did look long)? Or the layout? The words? What exactly?"

Sophie shows him an example, pointing to one she has opened and closed three times today.

- Capitals – there are a couple of instances which make Sophie feel the sender is shouting at her, almost instructing her what to do with no please or thank you.

- Spelling mistakes – this makes it hard to know what they really mean and gives a poor impression.
- No real structure - it jumps around from point to point.
- Length – it is so long that after about the third paragraph you lose interest.
- Closure – the sender didn't even have the courtesy to sign off with anything that remotely indicated they will appreciate help, let alone say goodbye politely. It felt like the kind of goodbye you receive when you have just been dumped by a boyfriend or walked out of a restaurant leaving no tip and they clearly don't want you back.

"All in all, I have no real desire to read the email and respond," says Sophie. "It's so poorly written and structured that it is actually very hard to really understand what is being asked and expected of me. In fact I wondered if the sender, a senior director, had written it either after having a blazing argument with someone or was drunk!"

That said, Sophie admits she has caught herself making some of these mistakes. She is looking to Max for guidance on just how to maintain the recipient's interest in her email and when questions are posed, respond to them all.

"That's very honest," says Max. "Yes, there are some basic guidelines, which will help you. They are no different from what you probably learned at school and later at university, albeit the rules of grammar have relaxed a little over the years. But we will come to that in a minute."

Email is a business record

In addition to your email being a picture of you, Max says it's important to remember that an email is a form of business communication. You may feel you know the sender well and that you are writing an internal email to a colleague with whom you get on well and have a developed a good working relationship. However, you don't know:

- What they will do with your email – maybe forward it to a colleague, client etc;
- How they are feeling at the precise moment they open your email. What you thought was funny they may not see in the same vein.

What you do know is that in all likelihood your email is being archived (kept) by the business for some time and maybe up to seven years. So let's have a look at some fundamental rules of email etiquette concerning the content (body) of the email.

Think in fives

Length is one of the reasons emails go unopened and unanswered, a point raised by Sophie in relation to some of the ones she too has left alone. Max says his golden rule is to **'think in fives' for the content:**

- Five sentences.
- Five short paragraphs.
- Five bullet points.

- Five questions.

"Any more than five and you are starting to write *War and Peace,* which is not what email is designed for," declares Max.

Email or a document?

"That's fine," says Sophie. "But people with mobile devices often don't like attachments." Max agrees but says that one can always either insert a summary or paste the content into the body of the email and remind the recipient that it would be better to read it when they are at their main device (laptop etc). The other point about using a document for a long communication is that you can utilise all the formatting functions and be sure that all your hard work is properly rendered by sending it as a PDF. Different email software often changes the formatting so that an email which you have perfected can look like spaghetti when the person receives it: this is especially the case for those using Lotus Notes rather than the more common Microsoft Outlook email client.

"Alternatively, if you want to keep to email, but it is starting to break the rule of five, split it into two separate emails," suggests Max.

Clarity and structure

Never use a long word where a short one will do.

George Orwell

Writing clearly is as important as the length. You must also take account of:

- Different levels of command of the English language (in global organisations, English may not be everyone's mother tongue).
- Mobile devices – with small screens it's important to make the emails easy to read.

Not surprisingly, Max has a simple template up his sleeve, which he says has worked well for many clients. It's the 'five Ss of email etiquette' for improving email communications and is shown below.

Five Ss for eye catching email content

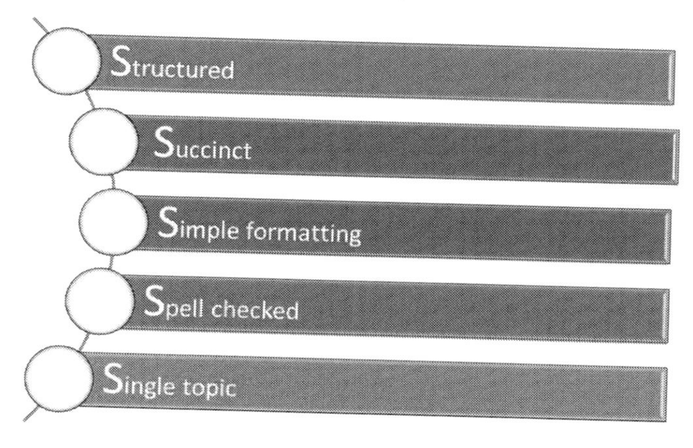

Use positive words as this gives a better impression of you. Avoid vague words and phrases, such as hopefully, maybe, sorry, in case, something, stuff, about, etc.

Structure

Key points here are:

- Newspaper style – give the recipient the headlines first (like an executive summary) just as you see with newspaper articles. This is especially helpful for those reading their emails on mobile devices.
- Flow – make sure your content flows properly and you don't jump from point to point.
- Guide the recipient through the main content to the conclusion.
- Make it easy for the reader to see the beginning, middle and end.

Succinct

Max says it's easy to get carried away writing an email and add unnecessary facts, flowery language etc. Good emails, he recommends:

- Keep to the point.
- Are factual.
- Use simple words and avoid any jargon and colloquialisms.
- Have a neutral tone and avoid any emotional words.

- **Minimise the use of unnecessary words, such as maybe, although, however etc.**
- Are grammatically correct.
- Include benefits to the recipient for responding as appropriate. For example, if you can send me the data as soon as possible, I can prepare your slides for you to review on your train journey on Thursday.

Grammar matters

Sophie comments to Max about grammar and how these days it seems people are more relaxed about it. "Fair comment," says Max. "I now see sentences ending with a preposition in anything from text messages to articles in the most respected newspapers and books, and even split infinitives."

Wrong	Right
Prepositions	
What is this extra meeting for?	For what (purpose) is this extra meeting.
Split infinitives	
We are going to in a minute break.	We are going to break in a minute.

George Orwell laid out six rules for effective writing, which have served many authors. Max offers these to Sophie.

1. Never use a metaphor, simile, or other figure of speech, which you are used to seeing in print.
2. Never use a long word where a short one will do.

3. If it is possible to cut a word out, always cut it out.
4. Never use the passive where you can use the active.
5. Never use a foreign phrase, a scientific word, or a jargon word if you can think of an everyday English equivalent.
6. Break any of these rules sooner than saying anything outright barbarous.

"The first five make a good starting point, while the last one is really your 'get out of jail card' for breaking the rules of grammar," says Max. "Formal writing can be hard to read, especially on a small screen. The key is to try to communicate clearly. Despite being a bit of a grammar nerd myself, you can write in a more relaxed style so long as your message is clear and you have reduced the margin for any misunderstanding."

The other most important element of good business communications is **don't use trivial phrases** like "so that's good", "Ok, here's the thing", etc. These are fine for social media and personal emails. However, by and large for business, it's better to stick to a more formal style.

With that they review a couple of emails Sophie has sent and she scores ten out of ten, unlike some of those she has received. Again, as Max re-iterates, by using good grammar and structure Sophie can set herself apart and make sure she stands out from the crowd in a positive way. She can also be a role model and in a nice way raise the bar for others with a more sloppy style.

Simple formatting

As mentioned earlier, when an email leaves your email system it may not look the same when received. Bullet points are often lost, the normal forms of formatting may be lost too, for example, italics.

Many people stick to either HTML or plain text for just this reason. However, you may not have a choice as the default template will be set by IT. In this case, where you have several points to make, the best option is to number them manually rather than using the numbering style format, which comes for example with Outlook.

Simple formatting also includes no unnecessary use for emphasis of:

- Capitals.
- Colour.
- Emoticons.
- Punctuation.
- Bold and italics.

Let your words do the speaking.

Spell checked

"May sound obvious but you would be amazed at the spelling mistakes I see in emails these days," says Max. "**Always spell check your email before sending it and watch carefully what the spell checker is doing with words that have multiple meanings** and especially homonyms (words with the same spelling but different meanings) and homophones (words with the same pronunciation but different spelling)."

Examples are shown below.

Homonyms	Homophones
Leaves	Buy/Bye/By
Foil	Morning/Mourning
Point	Their/There
Net	Principal/Principle
Rose	Grate/Great
Bow	Hail/Hale

Keep a watchful eye that the spellchecker does not change the word completely – for example, public to pubic, inconvenience to incontinence! "Again these little touches all add to the professionalism of your email and make it so much easier for the recipient to read and feel they want to respond," adds Max.

Single topic

"What do you mean by this?" Sophie asks Max.

"Well look at that previous email you have now opened for the third time. It has information relating to three different topics. So it's little wonder you are finding it hard to reply because the first item is simple – the time of the preliminary divisional meeting. However, for the second item you need to do some homework – what is the current response rate to the last social media adverting campaign."

"Now you have two options," he continues. "Reply to the easy questions and flag the email for further attention, or do nothing. Neither is very satisfactory as both risk the director sending a follow-up to re-ask about the outstanding questions. Furthermore in which folder does your response go? Also if you forward the email to the intern for help, you must be sure you have edited out the confidential information it contains about an employee."

Excellent email etiquette, Max suggests, dictates that where you have a series of different unrelated topics like this email, it is far better to split them into separate emails. Use the subject line to indicate that you are not spamming (thoughtlessly bombarding) the recipient. In the subject line put email 1 of 3, or however many there are, and then add the focus of each. This way they too can answer them more efficiently and promptly and tell you when to expect a reply to the ones that need more attention. "Focused *single topic* emails are also much easier to file and retrieve," he concludes.

"That explains why I often have to send chaser emails when I have included several topics all in one email. One topic will often be urgent, such as what time plane my director prefers, whilst other parts are less urgent, such as a list of speakers for the next away day. This is a process I will adopt now," says Sophie.

The action sentence

Begin with the end in mind.

Stephen Covey

"When we first started on email etiquette you said an 'action sentence' was the fourth one of the five key aspects of any good email. What did you mean by that?" Sophie asks Max.

"Oh that is easy," says Max. "Although it comes at the end, in many ways it should be the first part of writing the body or content of your email. It's akin to planning a meeting, you need to ask yourself what exactly is it you expect from the recipient? Do you need them to give you a response, confirm what you have said is correct, tell you what's the next step for them, and so forth? It makes you and the recipient focus even more tightly and reduces the need for follow-up emails to ask if they have read your email."

"Once you have written the email, whenever possible, include a question for the recipient – what I call a closing 'action sentence'," he adds.

"Now that is really neat," Sophie says. 'I frequently wonder what the sender is expecting from me and, conversely, wonder if they have read and digested what I send them. That is a real measure of whether or not they paid attention to what I wrote."

Review before hitting send

We are often so time poor that error creeps in simply because we hit send before reviewing what we've written. Max's slogan for email etiquette is '**Think before hitting send'**. This means:

- Review your email to make sure your message is clear and you have adopted the 'Five Ss of a good email'. This applies to all emails from two liners to five paragraphs. If in doubt, save it, take a break and re-review again before hitting send.
- When the recipient needs to respond, check you have provided sufficient information for them to make a decision.
- Where you are responding, check that you have answered all the questions the sender asked you.

This is the underlying principle of the **'slow email' movement, which allows time for everyone to think rather than seeing, sending and responding as a relay race**. Adopting these building blocks also reduces the rounds of email ping-pong as you have communicated *the right message, right first time.*

"OK," Sophie says. "I will take a little more time just as I do when dressing for a special occasion. From now on every email I send will be seen as special from the one sentence to the five paragraph ones."

Summary

- Every email you ever write on the business email address is a business record and may be kept for many years.
- Keep your emails short and think in fives. No more than five lines, five short paragraphs, five questions, etc.
- For long emails revert to a proper document writer (word processor) e.g. Microsoft Word.
- Structure and clarity are the king and queen of a good email. Use them to make it easy to maintain the reader's attention and make them feel drawn to respond to you.
- Use the Five Ss to help you write professional emails (whether new or responding):
    - Structure the content.
    - Be Succinct.
    - Keep to Simple formatting.

- Spell check before sending.
- Focus on a Single topic.

- Don't confuse the recipient by mixing your message and talking about multiple topics. If necessary split the emails and focus each on a specific topic.
- Good grammar is important but can be less formal if it makes it easier to read.
- When spell checking make sure the spell checker has not changed a word unwittingly so that the sentence no longer makes sense and especially with homonyms and homophones (words with the same meaning).
- Avoid sloppy phrases, colloquialisms and jargon.
- Practice the art of 'slow email' and leave time to review each and every email before hitting send.
- Always try to include an 'action sentence' at the end of your email to check that the recipient has understood what you have written.
- Imagine each email is special whether it's a one liner or longer. No matter the length, each conveys a picture of you and can either add or distract from the quality of the existing image the recipient has of you.

12

Completing your digital dress code – the closure

A man never knows how to say goodbye;
a woman never knows when to say it.

Helen Rowland

"What about the last part, the closure or sign off?" Sophie says to Max. "I see such a variety, from cheers, kisses, best and regards to nothing at all. Sometimes not even the person's name. Then there are those who include a line about the device from which the email is sent, as though it implies, 'I can be sloppy because…'

Indeed once I even saw one which said, 'Typos courtesy of my iPhone'. What are your thoughts on how best to close an email?" Sophie asks.

Closing to re-enforce the professional image

"A very important question," Max responds. "It is equivalent to the shoes that you wear. What is the point of taking time to do your make up, or personal grooming if you are a man, which is the email equivalent of your opening greeting – then putting on your best clothes, the content of your email, only to spoil it by wearing scruffy shoes? **The way you close your email is the finishing touch of your digital dress code.**"

There are some key dos and don'ts, which can broadly be assumed under the guideline of 'keep all the love and kisses for social email' and use a professional closure for business. Here are Max's preferred options and some examples of those that annoy most people most of the time.

Preferred closures for business emails	Closures to avoid in business
Best, best wishes (to someone you know well)	X, LOL, Hugs – all are absolute no-no's. Too informal and very open to misinterpretation. Best left for text messages between friends.
Regards	Smileys and emoticons. As above.
Kind regards, warm regards (common in the US)	Cheers – sounds like it's written with drink in hand.
Many thanks	Thx. Not everyone knows text speak.
Talk soon – warm and informal but professional	TTYS – same as above.
Your name – OK but can look terse	Sent from my iPhone. Can look arrogant and sloppy.

Forms of my name

"What to do about how I write my name?" asks Sophie. "Some people use an abbreviated version of their name (Dave for David when in the office they are called David)."

"This is all part of your digital dress code," explains Max. "Is the picture you conjure up for Mike different from that for Michael? Probably yes. So decide how you want to be seen in the eyes of the recipient and use that for your name. Nicknames are best left for social emails. You can use them for internal emails between colleagues you know well, but again remember you have relatively little control over what happens after you send the email. It might be forwarded to a senior director, external client etc. Then how are you perceived by that third party?"

Contact details, logos and all that jazz

In business you often have no say over the more formal aspect of how your emails are closed, that is your company signature block. Corporate communications, marketing, or a similar function will have laid down guidelines and probably provided you with a template signature block.

If you do have a choice, and you often do for internal emails, here are the four key items to include.

1. Full name.
2. Role/title to include the department within which you work.
3. Contact phone number.
4. Website (only for external emails).

"What about logos and strap-lines?" asks Sophie. "I see lots of emails with these and by and large they annoy me as they often take up more space than the content of the email."

"Agreed," says Max. 'Email is not the place to be marketing yourself and shouting about how wonderful you are. That's best left for the website and social media. Email when all is said and done, is simply a messaging system."

"The rule of thumb is **keep the signature block simple**," Max goes on to say. "Use the four key attributes above and you will not go wrong. People often wonder why email conversations go on for so long when everyone knows it would be easier to talk. One of the reasons is that no one has included a contact phone number. As we are all time poor (or sometimes just lazy) no one can be bothered to look one up."

Including a contact phone number is probably the single most important attribute in your signature block (after the closure). You must make sure this is on every email response you send, regardless of how many times you have responded and how long the email thread is getting. Why? Because, it may be after the fifth round of email ping-pong that the other person really wants to phone you, but is not prepared to search for it! Make it easy every step of the way. Indeed, this will encourage a phone call and stop those endless and pointless rounds of email ping-pong."

How many and which phone numbers?

"Brilliant," acknowledges Sophie. "But I am not letting you off the hook just yet. What phone numbers should I include, my direct land line, my mobile, and/or the main switch board?"

"Oh very good one – 15 all," says Max smiling. "Yes, you often see at least three phone numbers in a signature block. Very confusing. I recommend just your direct land-line. On the voicemail message you can always give the switchboard. But if the switchboard is not based in your office that might be a waste of time as they will have no idea of your whereabouts."

"If you give your mobile, it leaves you open to calls outside normal working hours. I only tend to give it to close colleagues and clients.

And one more point for readers working in small companies. Just having a mobile phone number smacks of a business being run from a garage. Yes I know that is how Apple and Microsoft started but they are the exception. I might be old fashioned but, for me, any serious business needs a proper land line. You can always divert it to your mobile, but remember the phone number is all part of your digital dress code."

"I had not thought of that way," responds Sophie. "Please can we stop for a minute, so that I can tighten up and shorten my signature block?"

"Go for it," replies Max.

Digital dressing complete

When I finish dressing before a night out and have put on all the accessories, I usually look at myself in the mirror long and hard and then end up removing something. Whether it's a belt, bracelet or a bauble, less is always more.

Joan Collins

After altering Sophie's signature, Max continues. "This completes your personal choices on how you deploy the rules of email etiquette to create the image you wish to convey of yourself. Just make sure Sophie, that when signing off (closing) the email, you do not destroy the virtual illusion you have so carefully created of you as a highly professional and organised yet friendly and approachable person, by a sloppy sign-off. Even with the shortest email, **think before**

you hit send and ask yourself, does this email convey the right image of me when it arrives in the other person's inbox? Have I brushed my clothes, straightened my hair, do my accessories (greeting and sign-off) match the overall clothes. No? Then edit and get it right, because you only have three seconds before the recipient forms their own opinion of you. Yes? Then hit send."

Priority markers and read receipts

Sophie has one last challenge for Max: "What about priority markers and read receipts?"

"Frankly when these appear on an email, that email goes to the bottom of my list," states Max looking disgusted. "They are arrogant and pushy. If you have written a good email with an excellent subject line then that will catch my eye and especially if you have put a date by when action is needed."

"OK." Max declares. "That said, I admit to using read receipts a few times, but as an exception and in particular when a problem is looming and I know evidence is needed that the email has arrived and been opened. For example, late payment, an employee is behaving poorly and disciplinary action is imminent. However, remember, an email opened does not mean it has been either read or understood. That is why an **action sentence is so powerful** because the response (or lack of it) tells you all you need to know."

"Time for a break," Max suggests and Sophie readily agrees. Off they march to the nearest place for a cup of real tea rather than the vending machine, which sometimes tastes of a mixture of tea, coffee and hot chocolate.

Summary

- See the words you use to sign off (close) the email as the finishing touches to your digital dress code.
- Use words that convey a professional image, such as many thanks, regards and best. You can use just your name but it might be perceived as curt and aloof.
- Leave all the social closures such as LOL, kisses and smileys for personal emails sent from your personal email, regardless of how well you know your business colleagues.
- Think carefully about how you use your name, and the image a shortened form sends, compared to the full version – for example, Sue versus Susan.
- Always include a contact phone number (no matter how many times you have already replied and long the email thread becomes), unless of course it is automatically included in the organisation's designated signature block.
- When you have a choice about the full signature block, forget all those logos and marketing slogans. Leave that to the website and the marketing materials.

13

Don't weigh your email down with excess baggage

The tempo is the suitcase. If the suitcase is too small, everything is completely wrinkled. If the tempo is too fast, everything becomes so scrambled you can't understand it.

Daniel Barenboim

By late afternoon, Max notices that Sophie receives some emails with several large attachments (5-plus MB). She often opens then closes them and leaves them in her inbox. Max also observes that about a third of her sent emails have attachments. On at least three occasions, Max watches Sophie update the file and resend it about half an hour later. On one instance she forgets the attachment completely. As it is for 20 people, Sophie has to send a rather sheepish follow-up with the file (meeting papers).

Why bother?

Max asks Sophie, "Have you ever been in that stressful situation when your mailbox is full and you can neither send nor receive emails until you downsize it?"

Sophie replies, 'Yes, which seems crazy to me that we have any kind of limit. After all the major free email providers give you gigabytes of mailbox space – for example, Google, Outlook and Yahoo, etc."

"That's true," says Max. "But in business it is very common for individuals to have a relatively small mailbox size (for example 100 MB). **Running large mailboxes carries an overhead for business, not least a cost and they can be unstable.** If the whole email system gets too bloated, it starts to run slowly and if there is an outage it can take more time to restore. Email outages are rare but do still happen. At one organisation everyone thought they could go home as they had forgotten how to work without email! To keep the email systems running smoothly, therefore, maintaining bandwidth and managing the risks of an outage, mailbox limits are often imposed."

Positive attachment management for those emails you receive and send means you and your division can:

- Stay within your mailbox limits.
- Avoid the pain (and stress) of being unable to send/ receive emails by being over the limit.
- Raise the green credentials.
- Contribute to managing the risk of a breach of security.
- Improve customer relations (internal and external).

Max continues. "Attachments are therefore the bane of not only most users' lives, but also most IT departments. They are the pariahs of mailbox and server space. Unmanaged you can easily find your mailbox is overcapacity in a matter of days. To counteract these challenges, many organisations implement document management and email archiving systems."

Indeed Max notices both in Sophie's organisation and asks if she uses either of them. "Sometimes. When I remember," she says cheekily.

Max gazes soulfully into his freshly brewed cup of tea. "Sorry Sophie, this was not meant to sound like a tirade but poor attachment behaviour is one of my *bêtes noires*. Working with limited Wi-Fi access and waiting for large attachments to download is like waiting for paint to dry. It is annoying and very customer unfriendly."

"Yes, that is not like you," says Sophie. "So tell me what you suggest. How can I and my colleagues better manage our use of attachments and especially avoid looking so silly by forgetting to attach files and waste time resending emails. Raising the green threshold is high on our corporate agenda."

Attach first then write the email

"This is my first principle of smart attachment management," says Max. "The last thing you do should be the first thing you do with an email. After you have sized and secured the file, **attach first then write the email**. This simple practice will significantly reduce the chance of you sending an email and forgetting to attach the relevant files."

Sophie looks quizzically at Max. "What do you mean sized and secured? Surely you have no choice about file size and earlier you said files are secure compared to the body of an email?"

Right size the files you send

I've learned that you don't need a lot in life.
If it can't fit into a suitcase, you don't really need it.

Joyce DiDonato

"Every organisation has a limited size of attachments that can be sent and received during the day to maintain the smooth running of their email systems. Generally this is about 10 MB. Some companies even impose very strict limits on the size of internal file circulation too (often around 2 to 5 MB). Otherwise imagine the impact of speed and bandwidth if four people each send you three 20 MB files one after the other. And believe me I have seen it happen," says Max. "Ironically, it's often from marketing professionals who feel that everyone must see an image in high resolution to appreciate it fully."

"Although," says Max shamefaced. "Once it was me who committed the felony: I sent my presentation to a conference organiser before checking the size. A few hours later there were frantic calls as to where was the file, as they were trying to load all the speakers' presentations. 'I've already sent it', was my response. Then I thought I'd check my sent items. Indeed I had sent it but it was 15 MB and hence sitting outside their main server waiting to be released in the evening. Fortunately the IT department released it on this occasion. Otherwise I would have had to do some downsizing myself."

Keeping the attachments small is essential. It is usually files with either images/photos or video that cause the problems. Here are Max's five essential ways to enable you keep your attachments small:

1. Check not just the original size but how it translates as an attachment. Look at the size shown in the attachment line.
2. Compress large files using one of the industry standards such as WinZip.
3. Locate the large images and reduce them (their resolution) and then reinsert them. If that does not solve the problem try splitting the file into two to three separate files bearing in mind they may have to be re-joined at the other end.
4. Use a file sharing service to which the file can be uploaded and a link sent to the other person. Internally this might be SharePoint, the Document Management system, even simply a shared network folder. For external use there are propriety applications such as Dropbox.
5. **Limit the number of files you send in one email (five is the maximum)** and always tell the recipient to what each file relates and where appropriate which files (and parts) are specific to them. The latter is especially relevant when sending out meeting papers. It helps ensure people attending the meeting are properly briefed.

Pull not push

"This will help you be seen as a good mailbox handler. These tips, and especially point five, help reduce email stress because you are in effect creating a 'pull' rather than 'push' email/information culture. The recipient can draw down the file when they are ready rather than feeling it is being thrown at them regardless of whether or not they want it, let alone download it easily," explains Max.

"This way too it does not matter if you send the file either to one or 100 people as you are not filling up mailboxes unnecessarily. Imagine if you send 30 people a 3 MB file which only ten people really need. What a waste of space and time as each person who does not need the file has to remove and delete it to keep themselves within limits."

Improved version control

Proper management of attachments is very much one of Max's hot spots. "Sharing links rather than files also means you don't fill up mailboxes, yours and the recipient's, with several copies of the same files because the file has been updated," he says. "Furthermore, you can control which version everyone sees by updating only the file that is uploaded and sending a new link (5 KB rather than 5 MB). That's a good way to make friends rather than enemies because no one likes a mailbox space hog."

Secure the attachment

"OK," says Sophie. "I have the sizing part, but what about the security aspects?"

"Unfortunately, attachments, although slightly more robust and private than the content of an email, still present an easy way to leak confidential information," explains Max. "For example, sending them to the wrong person and through the metadata contained in the raw file. In Word, you remove the revisions and edits but they have a habit of showing up again when sent out. In PowerPoint you can easily leave sensitive information in the notes pages, which are visible when opened. This once happened to Google and it knocked millions off their share price for a while because the data was about projected revenues."

Here are Max's top four key ways to improve the security of your attachments and again limit the risk of inadvertently leaking confidential information:

1. Clean before sending. Check you have removed any hidden columns in a spreadsheet, notes in a presentation, etc.
2. Send in PDF format as that removes any metadata especially in Word files.
3. Password protect the file (or use any other security functions available to you).
4. Restrict the recipient's ability to print and forward the file. Dramatic but sometimes very necessary.

"Limiting the number of people you include in the circulation list and send links, not raw files, also contributes positively to security. This reduces the number of copies in circulation should you need to recall it," adds Max.

Sophie says to Max, "In the age of social networking, many people have little regard for privacy and see it almost as a badge of honour to share everything with everybody. Transparency is imperative, especially after the Snowden affair. Yet it is clear that there are times when you want to protect information, perhaps it is because there is a sensitive sale in progress, take over, etc. These are useful tips. Thank you. I'd hate to be seen as the primary source of a leak."

Attachments on the move

I live out of my suitcase and I'm happy to do so.

Melanie Fiona

"Sometimes, a person will ask me not to send an attachment but rather paste the content into the body of the email, especially in the case for those constantly travelling," Sophie says. "Max, what's your view on this aspect of attachment handling?"

"First and foremost, you need to respect the other person's *modus operandi* and available technology. So do it, but send it also as an attachment so they have the complete file when they are back at their main PC."

"Second, you raise an important point, for those picking up their email on a mobile device," Max adds. "Attachments and especially long ones can be hard to read. An excellent tip to gain respect is to **send a very brief overview of what is in the attachment – like a Tweet just to give them a heads up** – and help them decide whether or not, and when, they need to read the full attachment (for example, before the meeting, at leisure etc)."

Don't duplicate the files you send

"One last very important matter about sending attachments," says Max. "Don't forget to always remove the attachments from the emails you send. These take up space in your mailbox and you of course already have them on your main document file. Remember too if you have a document management system you may need to send the file to that too. Otherwise you will become a real server space hog."

The attachments I send

Housekeeping ain't no joke.

Louisa May Alcott

"We have covered much on better attachment behaviour, but there is one last aspect that always perplexes me: what to do with the attachments I receive," says Sophie. "When I am over my mailbox limit, the quickest way to downsize is search for the large attachments (for example, over 5 MB) and save them elsewhere. Also sometimes my manager searches the document management system for a file and cannot always find it because it's still in my inbox! Depending on his mood and the urgency of the matter it can mean I am in hot water! How do I manage the attachments I receive to avoid these headaches?"

"There are a few simple principles of attachment housekeeping that will help you no end," replies Max. "The key is to ***do your attachment housekeeping little and often*** and preferably as you handle each email. If that's not always possible then do it at least a couple of times a week."

1. Always save the files you need to keep outside the email system in the folder to which they relate when you open the email (for example, project, event, person, client, etc). Then remove them from the original email.
2. Where you have a document management system make sure you adopt the correct procedures and again file them immediately in the system.

"These actions maximise the opportunity of being able to find files sent to you quickly and easily, and minimise the incidents of being over your mailbox limit," says Max.

Sharing attachments – sent and received

"During your career, Sophie, you will encounter many different email systems and procedures for handling attachments," Max continues. "Indeed, some argue that using a dedicated archiving application, such as you have now, negates the need to save and remove attachments outside the mailbox. That is true to some extent for individual mailboxes because most dedicated archiving software compresses the email as it archives it."

"However, where there is a strong sharing (collaborative) culture as you have in this organisation then it is most important that you file all attachments in the document management system. This means that not only can everyone access the file but it also ensures that everyone sees and uses the current version rather than an out-of-date one. I have seen so many instances of the latter and then the other person has to re-do any changes and, worse still, may be communicating out-of-date information to the client."

Sophie looks at Max and smiles. "Thank you. Now I understand why in business people are often neurotic about the management of attachments (both sent and received). Outside of business and using a proprietary email client such as Gmail this is not portrayed as an issue. With several gigabytes of mailbox space why should it? Also if I share files with friends it's via something like Dropbox or WhatsApp and confidentiality and version control are not high on our agenda. Although it makes you wonder just how environmental are such bulging personal mail boxes?"

There are just a few hours of the working day left and Max is conscious that Sophie needs to think about packing up her inbox ready for her vacation at the end of the week. Max also wants to address the issue of cybercrime.

Off for one last coffee break (and chocolate brownie) before they tackle these last two challenges. Although given it is 4.00 pm perhaps a peppermint tea is a better option to avoid any more caffeine.

Summary

- Attach first then write your email.
- Send links to, rather than actual files, particularly internally.
- Attachment housekeeping done little and often is best for both sent and received files.
- Adhere to the organisation's policy and procedures for managing attachments – for example, save them outside the inbox to an alternative such as a document management system.
- Clean and secure all and every file you send.
- Preferably avoid sending raw files. Rather use PDFs, especially for read-only files to external contacts.
- Be sure about any size limits on the files you can send during working hours (both internally and externally).
- Minimise the file size wherever possible.
- Limit the number of people to whom you send an attachment to both minimise hogging mailbox space and the number of copies in circulation.

- Be aware when sending attachments of those using mobile devices. Add a two-line executive summary to help the recipient decide what and when action is needed.

14

Be alert – keep yourself to yourself

If we don't act now to safeguard our privacy,
we could all become victims of identity theft.

Bill Nelson

As the day starts to draw to a close, Sophie asks Max about cybercrime and the fact that colleagues say email is often the easy back door for a hacker. She worries because it seems that even with state-of-the-art security technology, a hacker can still infiltrate your PC. For example:

- JP Morgan Chase was attacked in 2014 and lost 76m records.
- Sony in 2014 lost 10m records.
- Ashley Madison in 2015 lost 37m records.
- British Airways in 2015 had its frequent-flyer account hacked but said no personal data was lost.

In most cases, some of the records were emails, which exposed poor behaviour, libel, and personal data. In other instances, emails have been found where people have been disingenuous about their competitors and colleagues, and these have led to legal action and heavy fines. In the Ashley Madison instance, many people, both high profile and less ordinary mortals, are still concerned that over time details of their sex-life will be exposed.

"This is true," acknowledges Max. "Cybercrime now costs most organisations more than physical crime. **A recent UK government report estimated that cybercrime costs businesses at least £27 billion**. In addition there is all the mopping up and damage limitation when an organisation and its employees have been subject to cyber warfare. Cybercrime comes in many forms from having the email system hacked, in the Sony case, to highly sensitive information being accidentally leaked and simple identity theft."

"It is not just a hacker who can cause damage," Max continues to explain. "It can just be someone who forwards an email, which then goes viral; that company and the individual are then the stars of the next media email disaster. A good example is a receptionist who sent an all-user email about the arrival of the sandwich man and inadvertently used a previous email in which she had been discussing her love-life! In another instance a school girl received hundreds of unexpected emails because a Royal Naval Officer had accidentally included her name on a mailing list. She was then privy to some exceedingly confidential military information. There is a very important lesson here.

Always check you have sent the email to the right Jack Muggins."

"Very funny but very embarrassing," smiles Sophie, conscious that she just the other day sent one of the directors an email about Saturday's ladies golf competition. She had not carefully checked the address that had been automatically inserted when she started to type her best friend's name. No damage as the director replied in the spirit of the error suggesting he wore his kilt.

Cybercrime also covers breaking the laws that apply to human behaviour such as the Data Protection and Freedom of Information Act," Max continues. There are two fundamental points to remember:

- Emails can be used as evidence in court.
- We, the users, are the weakest link in the fight against cybercrime.

"Nonetheless, you can be the organisation's ears and eyes," says Max. "By adopting some basic principles of online safety, you can make a major contribution to the battle against the hackers and help reduce risks of a cyber-attack to either the business as a whole or yourself (for example, identity theft)."

"Tell me more," Sophie says to Max. "What are the early warning signs of an impending cyber-attack which I can spot?" Max suggests breaking it down into three areas:

- Basic precautions you must take with respect to the content of an email to stay within the law.
- Types of incoming emails, which should arouse your suspicions.
- How to ensure that your out-of-office message does not leave the back door open.

Stay within the law

Max explains that there are a number of laws that cover the content and use of email, and include:

- Data Protection Act
- Human Rights Act
- Computer Misuse Act

In essence, all three are designed to protect people's privacy and stop others from either disclosing private information or sending offensive information, for example jokes, racist comments etc.

These are Max's top seven tips to help you stay within the law and minimise the risk of either your email being used against you in a court case or seeing yourself as the star of the next media email-gate disaster.

1. Never write anything in an email that you are not prepared to say in person and defend in a court of law.
2. Avoid putting anything in an email that may be regarded as racist, discriminatory or defamatory about another person or organisation.
3. Do not send jokes that can be misinterpreted because what is funny to you might be offensive to someone from a different culture (be that religious or geographic).
4. Avoid swearing and blasphemy.
5. **Do not either blame or lambast another person via email when something goes wrong until you have first spoken to them**. Even then email is not the way to handle the situation.
6. When asked for an opinion on an incident, always preface your comments with 'in my opinion'. Do not make

your comments sound as though you are the voice of the organisation unless specifically asked to do so.

7. Only hold personal information about a colleague (or other business person) if either you have their permission or it relates to a current incident. In the case of the latter, delete the information once the incident is closed (for example, sick leave), unless of course you are legally entitled to hold the information as part of your job (for example, you are the HR director).

Max is emphatic: "If you have any doubts that what you are writing might jeopardise either yourself or the business, save the email as a draft and seek another person's advice. Often we make mistakes when writing in either haste or because we are angry. This is the time to practice the art of 'slow email'. Step back and leave the email in draft until you have a chance to reconsider your actions. This way you increase your chance of staying within the law."

"Most companies have an email security policy and sometimes even guidelines on what words you can and cannot use in an email. First, this reduces the risk of leaking confidential information and, second, limits any damage to the company reputation should emails be used as evidence in court."

Max urges Sophie to familiarise herself with both these policies.

Handling confidential emails to my manager

"Here is a situation I always find tricky," says Sophie. "When my director is out of the office and in long meetings, he expects me to keep an eye on his inbox in case of anything urgent and especially if anything comes in from his manager, the CEO. At least once a week, there is something sensitive and confidential. Sometimes I don't spot it in time and find myself reading something I'd rather not have seen – for example, redundancies, predicted sales figures for the quarter, latest research test results. My director trusts me implicitly and there is almost nothing that I don't know about. But sometimes I hear confidential information before even he has seen it."

"Max, what suggestions do you have which will enable me and my director to tighten up in this area of email security?"

"This is indeed a difficult one and an area where it is for the sender to be more savvy and security conscious," replies Max. "Here is a process that many of my clients use to protect both themselves and ensure their Assistant is not compromised by being privy to information that they should not and may not want to see. After all, you don't really want to know if your best friend is about to be made redundant before they know do you?" It's a three step process:

1. Ask all senders to mark emails which contain sensitive (confidential) information with the words 'confidential' in the subject line.
2. You then set up a folder on your director's inbox called 'Confidential'.
3. Write a rule to send all emails with the word 'confidential' in the subject line to that folder.

This will trap 99 percent of such email. In reality there will always be the odd one that slips through usually because the sender has misspelt the word 'confidential' or forgotten to include it in the subject line. Nonetheless this will greatly reduce the risk of you seeing such emails and hopefully make you feel more comfortable when managing Richard's inbox in his absence.

"I am going to email all the other directors. Then can we set up that rule on Richard's PC now as he is in a meeting?" asks Sophie.

Suspicious emails – be on your guard

Starts with a malicious email.

Kara Scannell and Gina Chon

Sophie quizzes Max further as she is now quite intrigued about the whole cyber-crime phenomenon, especially as her best friend recently had her identity stolen. Hackers accessed her friend's Facebook site and then her bank account. Fortunately the bank reimbursed her but at the time she was quite shaken by events.

"We have dealt with improving compliance and handling sensitive information," says Sophie. "But what about potentially suspicious emails, which can contain viruses? I thought our IT department had state-of-the-art anti-virus software, firewalls, and so on. How can anything nasty creep through?"

"Creep is a good word to describe hacking," says Max. He explains that a virus is really one of several forms of malware (although the terms are often used interchangeably). Malware is a small piece of software dropped into your computer by the hackers, which can infect it and/or make it behave strangely. There are four basic types of malware that can be disseminated through emails:

1. Virus – like a human virus, it infects files and emails you send but is less common these days.

2. Adware – which generates adverts on your computer screen usually by observing what internet sites you visit and then generating relevant adverts. Adware is more annoying than harmful.

3. Spyware – nasty stuff that does exactly what its name suggests. It can log your key strokes and then use the collected data to access your bank account, etc.

4. Worms – these again behave as their name suggest and worm their way into your files and destroy them. Again less prominent these days.

"There are other types of malware but these are the main ones and spyware is becoming the most common and invasive," says Max. "Yes, all should be detected at source by your anti-virus software but sadly sometimes they do creep under the radar. Perhaps either a client or friend has had their computer hacked and not realised. Before they know it, their computer then sends out suspicious email containing malware."

"In addition, there is straightforward hacking whereby the hacker gains access to the company's data by posing as an authentic person," adds Max. Typical suspicious emails have subject lines such as:

Your invoice….
Your delivery ….
X has sent you a link to...
HMRC tax return
Your XYZ account has been suspended
Mail delivery failed; or Undelivered Mail return to sender.
Invitation to connect on LinkedIn.

"In some cases, it is the havoc they cause by infecting machines," says Max. "In other cases, they are 'phishing' for personal information (as in spyware). They try to hook you by asking you to confirm aspects of personal data either via the email or more usually a fake website. However, take heart, being vigilant about which emails you open and links you click on can scupper many a cyber-attack perpetrated through email." Here are two crucial anti-cybercrime tips Max offers Sophie. **Never never, ever:**

- **Open a suspicious email** or at least the attachments contained therein. If you think the email is genuine, email the sender and ask them if they did indeed send you such an email. Invariably the response is no and, yes, their system has been subject to a cyber-attack.
- **Click on links in suspicious emails.** If you think the email is genuine, go to the web and access the site from there (for example, your PayPal or bank account). Often when a major site has been hacked it will have a warning notice on its home page.

The malware is usually contained in the link or the attachment. If you do perchance open the email, it's unlikely to cause any harm. Once you spot a suspicious email, always report it your IT/IS department. Some organisations have a special address to which you can forward such emails. Max recommends that Sophie check with her IT department what their preferred process is for dealing with such emails. Over the years Max has been involved in several damage limitation exercises due to cybercrime. "We can all be careless from time to time, but being always on your guard with unexpected and unusual emails can greatly reduce the risk of an email-predicated cyber-attack," says Max.

Passwords, passwords and more passwords

One other human factor security measure is to change passwords every so often. Indeed Max noticed at the start of the day that Sophie was being prompted to change her password by the end of the week. "I noticed that you ignored this," Max comments to Sophie.

"Hmm, yes, it is always hard to think of a strong password each time," replies Sophie. Max provides Sophie with two simple tricks of the trade:

1. Think of a place you have (or are about) to visit, then use that name and replace some alphabetic characters with numbers, for example a three for e and add a few special characters such as ! and *. To be even more robust you can change a letter in the middle from lower case to capital. Take Cologne where I was earlier this year. It can become CoLogn3!
2. Create a sentence that means something to you and use the first letter of each word and apply the principles above. For example I am going to Executive Secretary Live in Dubai 2016. This can become: IagtESliD16*.

"OK let's change my password now before the day end," Sophie says to Max.

Out-of-office message

This leads Sophie neatly to suggesting she starts to prepare for her week off and set her out-of-office message. "What are you planning to say?" Max asks Sophie.

"Something simple, like 'I am on leave from Monday 21 to Monday 28. If your email is urgent please contact one of my colleagues below. Otherwise I will deal with it on my return."

Max sighs. "That is not really very safe. You have opened two back doors. First, a cybercriminal can determine where you live within ten minutes and, hey ho, your house is burgled while you are away."

"You are joking?" Sophie intervenes.

"No, it's happened many times now. They are smart cookies today's cyber criminals. They are out to get all they can steal."

"Second," he continues. "You have revealed colleagues' email addresses, which the cybercriminal can now use for 'spear phishing'. That is to say, they can email your colleague with what looks like a genuine email from either you or another colleague and trick them into revealing sensitive information."

"My goodness," says Sophie looking aghast. "I had not realised that such dirty tricks were being played out there."

"Don't worry you are not alone. That is why cybercrime is on the increase and hard to contain at present," replies Max. "**Your out of office (OOO) message should reveal as little as possible about you and the organisation while being informative to the sender**." Here is Max's template, which adheres to this principle:

I am out of the office for the next few days, with limited email access. If your email is urgent, please call my colleague James Donut who will be able to help. Otherwise I will deal with your email when I am back in the office on X.

"This makes it just that bit harder for the cybercriminal because now they do not know if your house is empty or you are just on a course. So they move on to another OOO which gives away more juicy information. However, be warned," Max adds. "Even giving a person's name can lead to attempted hacking as one of my clients found. The hacker tried to pretend he was James Donut and that he had lost his security pass. Fortunately the telephone receptionist was on the ball and prevented what could have been a very costly disaster. In fact some clients do not even use the out-of-office message protocol now. Instead they ask each person to have a buddy who monitors their inbox in their absence. That's a thought for your return."

Meanwhile, for her forthcoming vacation Max helps Sophie set a simple bland message using the above template.

And when you are out of the office

Just before reviewing how to pack Sophie's inbox ready for her vacation next week, Max reminds Sophie how important it is to **be extra vigilant when accessing your emails and the internet outside the office** (and indeed your home). Top tips to guard your privacy and improve security are:

- Password protect your mobile device. Use the built-in functionality.
- Avoid using public networks to access personal financial data.
- Verify the name of the Wi-Fi that you are logging onto when in a public place such as a restaurant: ask someone when you see a list of names pop-up. Cyber criminals can easily set up bogus Wi-Fi networks and hence access your device.
- Be vigilant about who is around you. Cyber criminals can look like innocent by-standers also having coffee,

but in reality they can watch your keystrokes and, on an open public network, log into your device.

"Gosh, it's amazing what dirty tricks these hackers can play," exclaims Sophie.

"Yes and they are getting cleverer by the day," sighs Max. "However attention to all these small details goes a long way to reducing the risks and making their life more difficult."

Now it is nearly 5.00 pm and Max feels it is time to review Sophie's strategy for packing up her inbox ready for her holiday next week.

Summary

- Check carefully the names in the address list and make sure it goes to the right Lance Brown and Gillian White.
- Emails are permanent and can be used as evidence either for or against you. Make sure you stay within the law.
- Practice 'slow email' to avoid putting anything in an email that you might regret in time to come – for example defamatory, racist comments, etc.
- Avoid jokes too as these can easily be misinterpreted and cause problems.
- When dealing with your manager's email, make sure confidential emails are marked as such, and where possible filtered to a separate folder, which only the manager accesses.
- Be vigilant when you receive an email that is unexpected and looks in any way suspicious.

- Create strong passwords and change them regularly.
- When away from the office set a safe and simple out-of-office message that discloses the minimum of information about either you or others in the organisation.

15

Take leave of your inbox

For me, holidays are about the experiences, and the people, and the memories, rather than sitting on a nice beach getting tanned. I try to plant myself where I am and embrace what is there in front of me.

Evelyn Glennie

To connect or disconnect while on leave?

The day is drawing to a close and Max remarks how enjoyable the day has been with Sophie. "You are not alone in the challenges you face to reduce the level of email traffic through your inbox. One client says he has about 100 emails a day of which he probably only needs 20. The volume of unwanted emails can be very forbidding after taking time out of the office and especially a week's vacation as you will at the end of the week."

"Yes," chips in Sophie. "We have no vacation policy about whether to stay connected or disconnect from the office email. Although Richard the MD and my manager are encouraging us all to **take the *Email Free Vacation Oath*.**"

"Tell me more," says Max.

"Well the Email Free Vacation Oath is a commitment to disconnect and stay disconnected from work emails while on holiday."

"That is a fantastic step forwards and just what I'd expect of an organisation that has well-being as one of its core values," says Max. "What is stopping you then?"

"Primarily the backlog of emails that will be waiting for me on my return. And my own will power," replies Sophie. "We have a Bring Your Own Device (BYOD) policy so my iPhone (and iPad) double as my personal devices and also devices of choice for checking work emails when away from the office."

Max fires back by asking Sophie what she has done in previous years (and at her previous organisation). "Checked them of course," says Sophie looking rather soulful.

"I am not surprised you have just lost your smile and your shoulders are dropping," says Max.

"Let's put things in perspective," Max continues. "To stay connected or disconnected while on holiday is a dilemma that many people face. On the plus side, you stay on top of your inbox and colleagues may envy how you look so important and responsible. Or do they? We are none of us indispensable. In this age of supposed 24x7x365 business there is a temptation to think the organisation will grind to a halt if we don't make ourselves available constantly, which means checking our emails wherever we are. However, **we all need to re-charge our batteries from time to time**. Working long hours is to some extent a very British (and perhaps US) habit. An intense working life is not always good for personal relationships and indeed our well-being."

Moreover, a recent National Survey of Sexual Attitudes and Lifestyles (Natsal) found that as laptops and mobile devices make their way into the bedroom their owners are enjoying less sex than a decade ago. The number of days off due to stress-related conditions has risen over the past three years and now costs UK business about £70 billion each year in lost productivity.

Not surprisingly, an increasing number of organisations are taking the impact of email overload on well-being and the work-life balance very seriously and finding ways to help staff at all levels switch off and have a proper break. For example:

- Daimler Benz introduced an email programme which automatically deletes all employees' emails while they are on leave. It tells the sender this is happening and asks them to re-send any important emails on the recipient's return from leave.

- Digital detox holidays are now on offer. When you arrive at your hotel you can elect to have all Wi-Fi connections disconnected.

- Volkswagen has stopped all email traffic going to non-executives after 6.30 pm each day.

- At one of Max's clients, the MD does no meetings after 5.30 pm and leads by example by stopping work then too. When in the office he challenges those still working.

- In France and Germany they have introduced legislation to stop those in the 'digital and consultancy' sector from being forced to receive emails outside normal working hours (roughly 9.00 am to 6.00 pm).

"With that in mind, Sophie, how did how you feel last year when you checked your emails on vacation?" asks Max.

"Not happy. On one occasion it disrupted the morning's plans, as it took so long to deal with the email. At other times, I felt that just as I was relaxing, my whole body would tighten up when I saw how many emails were coming in and especially if one annoyed me."

"Well Sophie, I think you have the answer going forward," smiles Max. "And especially as your MD is encouraging you all to take the Email Free Vacation Oath."

"OK, and especially as I know my partner hates it when I log in. For the sake of our relationship I have been known to sneak off to the bathroom to have a quick look! But before you go, please, please will you give me some advice on the best way to pack up my inbox for leave and how to sort it quickly on my return?" asks Sophie.

"Let's get started," replies Max.

Pack your inbox ready for a vacation

Max explains that there are four main considerations to packing up your inbox before taking a break:

1. Clean out your inbox before your leave – how and when.
2. Prioritise what emails you will want to see on your return and what can be automatically foldered.
3. Brief the colleague who is monitoring your inbox (and your managers).
4. Decide what to say on your out-of-office message.

"We have laid the foundation for some of the points in previous chapters, so let's pull together the principles in relation to having a break. That break may also just be taking time out to attend a conference, training course, etc," says Max.

Clean out your inbox

"**You want to make sure you clear out all the old emails, which are now long past their sell-by date**," says Max. Here is his quick four-step process to reach inbox zero – or at the very least leave just a few emails in the inbox for your return.

Five steps to packing your inbox for a vacation

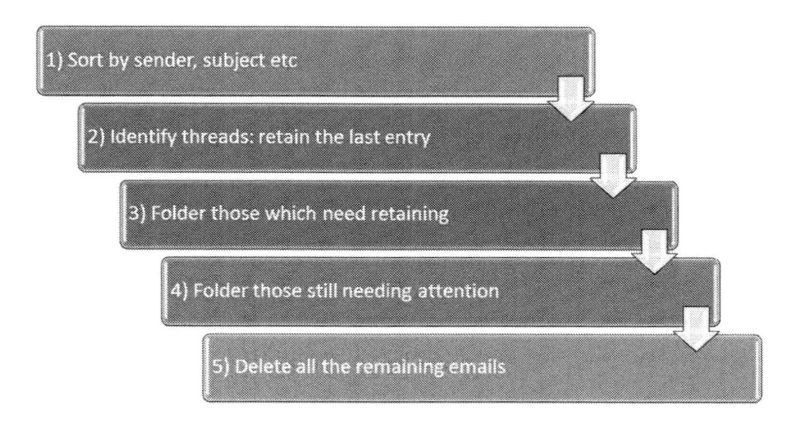

"If you don't quite have the courage to delete all the irrelevant emails, then at the very least move those out in to a separate folder (called, for example, Old Jan to Jul 2015)," says Max.

"For emails which still need attention, either leave them in the inbox or better still move them to a folder for action on your return.

How long the clean-up exercise takes will of course depend on how many old emails you have and how ruthless you can be," he adds. "Usually, I'd suggest leaving an hour for a few days during the week prior to going away. To make sure it happens make an appointment with yourself in your calendar."

Prioritise what enters your inbox

"Apply exactly the same principles we discussed earlier [see Chapter 3] to help you see the wood for the trees on your return," says Max. "Decide what emails you must see and what can wait. Then use rules to filter out to folders all the second-order priority emails – for example, newsletters, circulars, etc."

Brief the colleague looking after your inbox

Max is a great believer in give and take. "**Buddying up with a colleague so that you can look after each other's inboxes when one of you is away is a valuable practice**. Some people, I acknowledge, dislike this approach because they feel someone else can see all their personal emails. As you will see, however, it's easy to adopt measures to ensure a relatively high level of privacy."

Indeed Max remembers that Sophie said it was customary for the Assistants to buddy up and watch over each other's inboxes when one of them was on leave. This also extends to keeping an eye on the other director's inbox that the Assistant looks after.

Max tells Sophie that she needs to leave time to brief her colleague Charlie who is going to oversee both her own inbox and Richard's when she is on leave. Specifically Max insist that Sophie briefs Charlie about:

- Current projects in hand (for herself and Richard).
- Emails Sophie and Richard are expecting relating to key clients and projects (based on the above) and which might need attention – if only a holding response.
- How to deal with Richard's inbox, what he likes and dislikes, how they alert each other to important emails and what action has been taken and how they manage the calendar. Max also points out that Sophie must check that the rule for handling 'confidential' email is switched on and working.

Additionally, before going, Sophie needs to create a folder (and related rules) for social/personal emails from friends and family. This will maintain privacy for Sophie. Although her organisation discourages people from using the business email for private and social purpose, they are allowed to make limited use of it.

"Too often people delegate inbox access to others and then expect them to somehow read their mind as to what is needed," says Max. This is *mushroom management* and it is little wonder that when the key person is away either mistakes happen and important emails are missed or conflicting replies are sent. All these risks can be minimised by leaving sufficient time to brief Charlie. "And while you are at it,' Max says, "*make time immediately you are back for a de-brief* with Charlie."

At this point Sophie stops to schedule a 30-minute meeting with Charlie for later in the week and early on her first day back. (This takes a few minutes as she checks

Charlie's availability using the calendar scheduler to find a mutually convenient time.) Fortunately, because Sophie is planning ahead, Charlie is free at 9.00 am on her first day back.

Setting the out-of-office message

Bad news isn't wine. It doesn't improve with age.

Colin Powell

Max reminds Sophie that they have created a simple and safe out-of-office (OOO) message [see Chapter 14]. In addition, Max says it is sensible time management to set it for one day before and one day after you actually leave and return to the office. "This gives you time to clear both your desk and inbox and then catch up," he says. "I always keep the day before and after leave, meeting free."

Sophie remarks that these days several colleagues write a rule that deletes all their emails and sets an OOO message saying so.

I am away from the office from X to Y. All my emails will automatically be deleted during this period. If your email is important, please re-send it on my return. Meanwhile if your email is really urgent please contact Charlie who will try to help you.

Max smiles wryly. "Yes, over the years, I have observed many people take this route with internal emails. It has become even more popular following the trend set by Daimler in 2014 with its 'Mail on Holiday' programme. It is to counter the volume of unnecessary internal emails, which by the time the person returns, have become irrelevant – for example, the problem has been solved, meeting passed, report written, leaving party happened etc. It is a form of 'email bankruptcy' and a very effective way to reduce the email vacation stress and need to stay connected. It also means you return to inbox zero."

"Yes, but what will clients think?" Sophie asks, looking perplexed.

"Many email applications offer the option to write at least two out-of-office messages," Max says. "One is for internal and the other for external emails. Furthermore, you can be very clever and add exceptions – for instance, for emails from certain people, like the CEO. On balance this approach is excellent for those who do not have a buddy to whom they can delegate their inbox when on vacation. I have seen some very senior business people take this route and I too have used it," says Max. "It is something to discuss with Richard as part of your Email Free Vacation programme."

Nonetheless Max recommends to Sophie that as she has Charlie to oversee her email, she just writes a simple and safe OOO like the ones discussed earlier, but sets the date for one day before and after her vacation.

"I really like that suggestion," says Sophie. "It'll give me a day to tidy up all the loose ends and one to get up to speed on my return before being involved in any meetings."

On vacation

What if you feel you really must access your inbox while on vacation? Perhaps, your colleague has called and asked your advice on a time critical project? **Try to check your emails only at the end of the day and allocate a limited time to do so.** This will cause the least stress and disruption to your holiday plans even if they only involve lying in the sun with an Amaretto Sour.

Banish the post-holiday inbox blues

It is far more difficult to murder a phantom than a reality.

Virginia Woolf

"So Max, it looks like I am all sorted to disconnect for my holiday. But what about the inbox bombshell, which will be awaiting me on my return?" asks Sophie. "That's the part that really gives me goose bumps the day before I am due to return. Once there were just under 1,000 new emails after taking two weeks off. It took me nearly a week (on and off) to reduce the inbox down to just 30, which were important and needed on-going attention."

"Elementary," says Max, and shows Sophie a five-point process that has worked time and again for his clients. He promises it will take away all the stress and help Sophie restore order to her inbox quickly.

Five steps to unpacking your inbox after a vacation

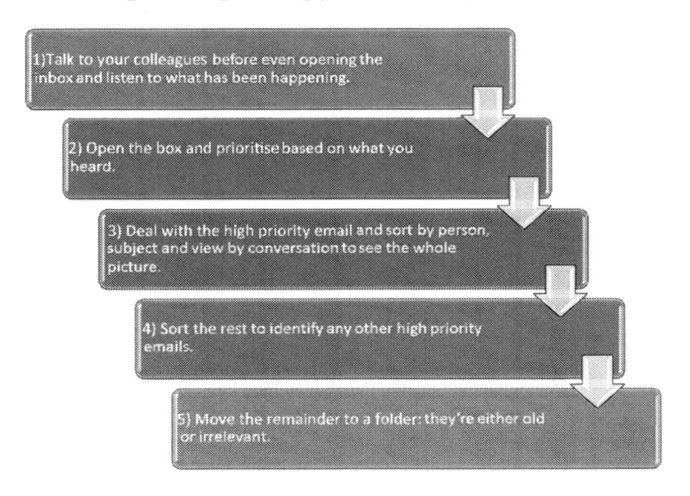

Talk, talk and talk again

"By now as you might expect, the key is to use your ears and eyes to see the big picture of what has happened while you have been away rather than get lost in the minutiae of your inbox," says Max. "Furthermore, diving straight into your inbox immediately after you arrive at the office will give you a very blinkered view and, if you are not careful, waste your time (yours and the recipient's) dealing with emails that are no longer relevant."

"One Assistant (Anna) knew I liked to arrive really early on my first day back," explains Max. "She would leave me a one-page briefing note on major happenings, which emails needed my immediate attention and what action she had taken in respect of them. Sometimes, if Anna had time, she sorted them into four main folders." They would be marked:

- Immediate attention.
- Attention during the first day.
- Meeting related.
- For information.

"I have seen others use colour categories for the same purpose," he adds.

Sophie acknowledges that this is something for her to discuss with Richard. "That would certainly help Richard on day one because he usually arrives really early to catch up with overseas colleagues and especially our Australian office," she says.

Open the box, prioritise and re-sort

"Well," declares Max. "If you set some filters before going on leave obviously this should have removed a high percentage of the lower order priority emails. When you finally open your inbox, it should mainly contain emails of significance and they could well amount to several hundred if you have been off for a couple of weeks."

"The trick now is to cluster them by person, project, type, etc, and at the same time view them in thread/conversation mode," he adds. "That allows you to see the whole conversation but with the latest one first. Then you can decide how to respond (if a response is still necessary). Using this conversation/thread view one Assistant told me she then deletes all the duplicate emails which just leave the one email containing all the discussion."

Max adds that it is also useful to move immediately certain types of emails out – for example, meeting invitations (formal and informal). "You then review these later when you have a clearer picture of what lies ahead."

Max explains that some people (especially senior executives) sort by where their name appears. "They only look at those emails that have their name in the 'To' box on the basis that if their name is in the 'Cc' box, it's for information only. Indeed quite a few people have permanent rules which automatically sends all their Cc'd email to a separate folder, which they only review once a week, as discussed before."

"That's a great approach. There is only one problem," says Sophie.

"What's that?" asks Max.

"Some people put me in the Cc line when writing to Richard and then expect action from me," replies Sophie.

"Ha, you know from our previous discussion how to change those senders' behaviour don't you Sophie?" exclaims Max.

"Hmm, just wait until they ask why I have not actioned their email," Sophie says laughing.

"Absolutely," says Max. "They must write to you and Richard with both your names in the 'To' line."

"You could do the same if they have written to you on an old email but about a new subject and hence when you sort using either the conversation view or subject you might miss their email! That's why it usually pays to sort the inbox a couple of times using different criteria," adds Max.

"Just remember whatever approach you take, be decisive," he says. "Use the 4Ds principle [see Chapter 2]. **Always do something with each email as you open it, even if it is only to delete it. If there are emails about which you are unsure whether they are relevant, create a 'Pending' folder into which these go once you have read them.** Don't leave yourself with a sea of half-opened emails one hour after you have opened the box. Otherwise cleaning up takes twice as long and makes it feel even more stressful."

Move the rest to a folder

"What about all the other lesser priority emails?" Sophie asks Max.

"Simple," replies Max. "After a couple of days (at most), move all the remaining emails out of your inbox into a separate folder (called maybe 'August 2015 left overs'). Now you will at least have a clean inbox and perhaps even reached the Holy Grail state of having an empty inbox. **If you have missed anything, you can be sure the sender will re-send in a few days once they realise you are back and have not responded. When this does happen don't feel guilty**. Take a careful look at the original and try to identify why it was missed."

- The sender may have committed one of the email sins we just discussed (you are in the Cc box or the subject line is misleading). In this case when you reply, indicate how to avoid this happening next time.
- What is their high priority might not be so high for you. Again find a polite way to convey this information. It might be that you no longer need such emails in the first place. Ask to be taken off the circulation list.

No approach to sorting a large backlog of emails is 100 percent foolproof. However, adopting a five point process like this one will help you save time and spot 95 percent of the important emails."

Email bankruptcy

Today, certain people file for bankruptcy, businesses and individuals, and it no longer has the stigma it once had. Now it's almost considered wise, a way to regroup and come back again.

David Dinkins

Max explains to Sophie that people have been known to declare email bankruptcy and just delete the whole lot. "It takes courage and it gives you the opportunity to wipe the slate (inbox) clean and re-think your priorities unencumbered by the backlog of unopened and often unanswered emails. For those who ask why you have not responded to their email, it is making a very bold statement to them about taking more care and avoiding filling up people's inbox with unnecessary emails," extols Max.

"Yes, I have read about such approaches," smiles Sophie. "Not sure I can do it here, but I do it with my personal emails sometimes. And I have never yet missed an important dinner, game of golf, invitation, etc."

"Sophie," Max announces. "You are clear for take-off." With that he vanishes. Sophie looks around, goes to the kitchen, and then the café. But there is no sign of Max.

It is now 6.00pm and Sophie's Pukka Pad Project Book is chock full of notes about email best practices to improve productivity. She decides to leave for a quick drink with friends before going home.

She has four days before going on leave during which time she will reflect on her day with Max and make some plans for how to improve the way she manages both her own and Richard's inbox over the coming months.

Summary

- Take the Email Free Vacation Oath and disconnect from your inbox while on leave. This will improve your wellbeing and productivity when you return to work. It will also help you enjoy your vacation and improve personal relationships that can be strained when both partners have demanding jobs.
- Allocate quality time before going on vacation cleaning out your inbox.
- Write rules to filter out automatically all non-essential emails (for example, newsletters).

- If you manage someone else's inbox (for example, your executive's) make time to brief properly the colleague who is monitoring it (and yours) in your absence.
- Set a simple and safe out-of-office message and date it for one day before and after your leave. This leaves time to clear your desk and then re-acclimatise on your return.
- On your return, before going anywhere near your inbox, talk to colleagues to establish what are the real priorities for the next few days.
- When you finally open the inbox, prioritise the email by sorting by subject, type (for example, meeting invites), Cc versus To, sender, etc. Use the conversation view to group the threads (chains) of email discussions and delete all old entries in a thread.
- Apply the 4Ds principle to make sure you do something with each one (even if it's only to move it to a folder).
- Two days after your return, move all the remaining emails out of the inbox to a folder to give yourself an empty inbox.
- Consider declaring email bankruptcy, if three days later you still have a full inbox.
- Do not worry or feel guilty about emails you miss because the sender will soon re-establish contact if the matter is important. Also the sender either might not have made it that easy for you to spot their email or their priorities may not be yours.
- If you do feel you need to check emails on vacation, then do so only once and at the end of the day.

Epilogue: going forward

The next morning, before Sophie even switches on her email, she reviews all the notes from her time with Max the day before. She decides to highlight the actions she will take in relation to:

- Her own inbox.
- How she works with Richard to manage his inbox.
- How they (she and Richard) might improve the way the whole sales division uses email.

Sophie by herself

In addition to the changes she has already made with Max's help, she decides to immediately take the following five actions:

1. Audit the incoming emails and be ruthless about what she really needs and what is unnecessary. She takes herself off mailing lists (where she can), and otherwise writes a rule

to move the unnecessary emails to the deleted folder. For less important emails, but which she still wants to see, she writes rules to move them automatically to folders.

2. Have 'email free Friday afternoons' when she will endeavour to answer at least all internal emails by either walking to see the sender or calling them.

3. Always carry her Pukka Pad Project Book when she walks around the office. Although she has an iPad, writing in her notebook is often quicker. She is also not tempted to check her emails and hence be distracted. When asked to do something, she will immediately make a note, instead of asking the other person to send her an email.

4. Adopt the slow email principle, and wait both to check and answer her emails and re-read them before sending them.

5. Stop checking her work email after 6.30 pm and not re-check it until she arrives at the office the next day.

Sophie and Richard

Sophie makes quality time to discuss with Richard how they manage his inbox. While they agree to keep to the current system for managing Richard's emails they will:

- Make more use of texting to alert Richard of urgent emails needing his attention.
- Review where there is duplication and tell the sender to remove one of them (for example, meeting invites).
- Remind all the other directors and their Assistants to put Sophie in the 'To' address box when action is expected from her.

The division

Improving the way emails are used is already on the agenda as about half the team have cited email overload as an issue in their appraisals. They decide that when Sophie is back from her email free vacation they will:

- Draw up and launch an Email Best Practice Charter for their division to cover aspects such as email etiquette, when to use an alternative to email, acceptable response times and having email free periods.
- Based on their Email Best Practice Charter, run some workshops and webinars, as part of their 'Well-being' and their 'Going Green' weeks.
- Have a couple of fun events to help people change their email behaviour, where money will be raised for their charity of the year – for example, no emails within a five-desk radius. Anyone who breaks the rules is fined.
- Install three whiteboards in their office space and use them for transient messages for which no record is needed (for example, fire alarm test, drinks to celebrate a birthday, new coffee machine, etc).
- Make sure everyone has a notebook to hand.

Sophie decides they will need advice from an external consultant to help improve how email is used across the division. Richard agrees to a budget and says that if they are successful they will go companywide the following year. In effect, her division will be the guinea pig, and pilot the Email Best Practice Charter.

Sophie thinks often of her day with Max on her return from leave. And, as the weeks progress, reviews her notes and adopts one new piece of best practice every two or three weeks. Once she thinks she sees Max with a colleague, but how could she, given Max is only visible to the person being coached?

Over the next six months everyone notices a significant fall in the volume of email traffic (for some up to 50 percent less) and improvement in communications. There are far fewer misunderstandings, leaving only small exchanges of crossfire, which are easily extinguished, rather than full-blown email wars.

About 75 percent of her division take the Email Free Vacation Oath and adopt the Email Buddy principle, pairing up with a colleague to keep an eye on each other's inbox while they are on leave. Everyone feels less stressed and less need to stay connected 24x7x365.

By the end of the year they are voted 'Division of the Year' as the best place to work in the organisation.

Quite a return on Sophie's investment of a day spent with Max learning how to manage her inbox more effectively.

Acknowledgements

Alone we can do so little; together we can do so much.

Helen Keller

The great American writer Ernest Hemingway once said, "There is nothing to writing. All you do is sit down at a typewriter and bleed." To some extent that is true. However, writing is also a lonely process and without the advice and support of a few friends and colleagues, this book may never have been written. I wish to thank the team who helped make this book a reality rather than just a dream and especially those mentioned below.

Executive Secretary Magazine - I am exceptionally grateful to the team at *Executive Secretary* and especially Lucy Brazier for inspiring me to write this book as part of her *Executive Secretary* set of handbooks for Assistants, to Caroline Poynton for patiently editing the copy and Matthew Want for stepping up in Lucy's absence.

www.executivesecretary.com

Pukka Pads – as the daughter of a long line of traditional stationers and printers my love of pen and paper endures. Pukka Pads have been a wonderful sponsor keeping me in the manner to which I am accustomed. I am most appreciative of all those executive pads on which to map ideas and paper for print drafts. It is still easier for many of us to review documents on paper than on screen. Thank you too for your input to the content.

www.pukka-pads.co.uk

KPMG – for allowing me to re-use self-help material written for them for their intranet and especially to Martine Marshal for being a sounding board about how exceptional EAs work with exceptional executives. Thank you.

www.kpmg.com/channelislands

Bourne-Fit – to Si and Luke, a big thank you to you both for your input on well-being and keeping me physically fit. The pain has been worth the gain.

www.bourne-fit.co.uk

Sue France – for so kindly writing the foreword. Always ask a busy person when you need a job well done.

www.suefrance.com

Lorna Campbell and Susan Oakes – both have been part of the Mesmo Consultancy team for many years. Their dedicated eye for detail and checking of chapters goes well beyond the call of duty. I am indebted to you both for your support.

www.mesmo.co.uk

Pearson Education – for permission to include material from *Brilliant Email.*

www.pearsoned.co.uk

Clients and colleagues – thank you all for enriching this book with your many tips and anecdotes given generously in workshops, coaching sessions, webinars and emails.

As a golfer, one never, ever blames oneself for shots that drift off the fairway and fall in strange places and the putts that just don't drop in the hole. Writing this book provided me with endless excuse for such mishaps on the course. I thank all my many playing partners for putting up with these strange shots.

Now a new project will have to be found on which to blame my sometimes less than perfect play!

More resources and information

Thank you for taking the time to read this, my third book on email best practice. I trust you enjoyed reading it and benefitted from the tips in it. By now you are maybe thirsty for more advice and tips for yourself and to share with your colleagues.

You will find plenty of extra resources on the Mesmo Consultancy website at www.mesmo.co.uk. For example:

- On-line self-assessment tools:
    - Email etiquette.
    - Email addiction.
    - Cost of unnecessary emails.
    - Outlook Fitness.
- Videos.
- Workshops, masterclasses, webinars and one-to-one coaching.
- Blogs with tips and articles of note.

- E-briefing – our monthly e-newsletter, which you can sign up to either from the website or email your details to info@mesmo.co.uk.

You can also find me on the usual social networks where I regularly post material and news on email best practice:

@EmailDoctor

Brilliant Email

Monica Seeley

I am always delighted to hear from readers like yourself with both your questions and your personal tips. Please do contact me:

Tel: +44 (0)1202 43 43 40

Email: info@mesmo.co.uk

Dr Monica E. Seeley

About the author

Dr Monica Seeley, founder of Mesmo Consultancy, is an international expert on email best practice. Monica enables organisations and individuals to manage their use of email more effectively to improve business and personal performance and communications. Through her one-to-one coaching, workshops and strategic consultancy, those who work with her are able to save time and dramatically reduce email overload, which has become one of the major drains on people's productivity.

Her clients are drawn from a wide range of organisations of all sizes from the public, private and not-for-profit sector. Over the past fifteen years she has coached and trained thousands of business executives, at all levels in the organisation and from a wide variety of roles including CEOs, finance directors, warehouse managers, sales personnel, marketing, engineering, Assistants, EAs and receptionists.

Monica is a Visiting Fellow at Sir John Cass Business School, City University and Bournemouth University Business School. Her research includes the future of email and the use of social technology to improve communications.

The media frequently seeks her opinion on the effective strategic use of electronic communications and especially email. She frequently contributes to BBC programmes and the *Financial Times* and has her own blog page on Huffington.com.

She has written many articles and several books on email best practice including the popular *Brilliant Email*. As the @emaildoctor on Twitter, Monica posts daily tips on smart email management and her Brilliant Email Facebook site also contains a wealth of resources.

Monica Seeley

brilliant Email

How to win back time and increase your productivity

Made in the USA
Columbia, SC
14 May 2017